JOURNEY TO ALLAH SERIES

WHAT IS YOUR BELIEF?

A PRACTICAL GUIDE TO KNOWING ALLAH

All thanks are due to Allah subhaanahu wa ta'ala for enabling us with this effort.
Special thanks to the following contributors:

Content Writers: Umm Eesa and Dalia Elamawy
Islamic Studies Curriculum Editing Team: Amber Bokhari, Br. Abdul Qaadir Abdul Khaaliq, Samira Hingoro
Graphic and Layout Design: Farah Firman

A project of Dar-us-Salaam community, College Park, MD, USA
www.darussalaam.org

2nd Edition

Printed in the United States of America

ISBN 979-8-9874006-5-4

For permission requests, write to the publisher at the address below.

FAITH Publications
5301 Edgewood Road
College Park, MD 20740, USA
Phone: 301-982-9848
Email: iscurriculum@alhuda.org
faithpublications.org

TABLE OF CONTENTS

UNIT 1 | FINDING PEACE

UNIT 2 | INTRODUCTION TO OUR CREATOR

UNIT 3 | ALLAH IN MY LIFE

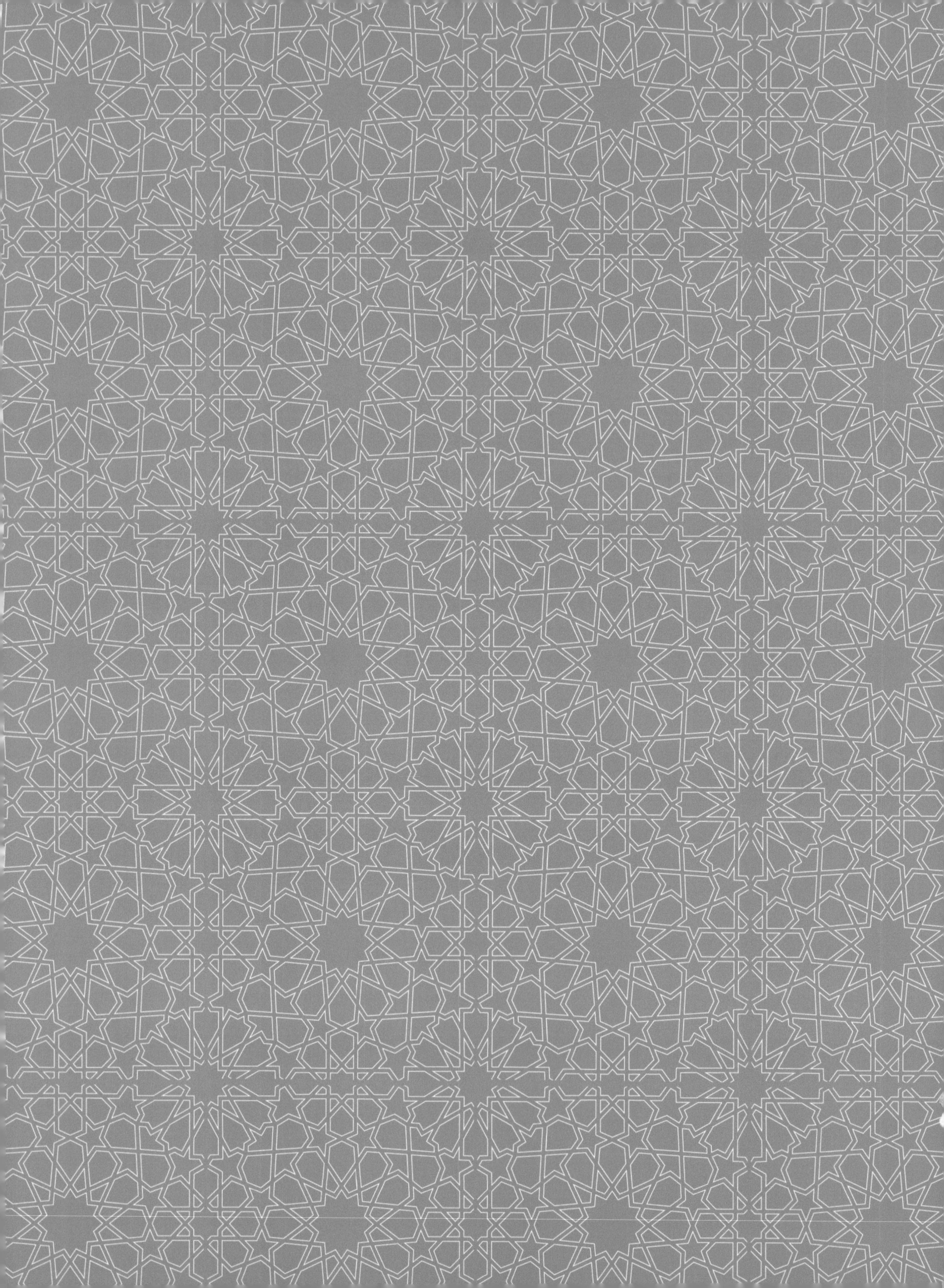

PREFACE

We live in a rapidly changing world where conflicting views and opinions shape how we see the world and how we see ourselves. With information overload comes confusion and stress, especially for young people who are amid self-discovery. Young people like you.

Now more than ever, it is imperative for high school students to have complete certainty in Islam. Our belief system has been meticulously preserved for over fourteen centuries, and our faith always proved its truth when challenged by every man made ideology. A proper understanding of your faith will anchor you in today's world of doubts, disbelief, and self-centeredness.

This is an introductory book on Islamic belief that explores how our emotional wellbeing connects to our relationship with our Creator: Allah. It provides answers to some frequently asked questions: *What is the purpose of my existence? Why am I here? Why do I need faith to be a good person?*

After having countless conversations with young people who asked these same questions, we wrote this book. We have seen what happens when they get answers. This book will help you begin your journey to know Allah, and that journey will transform the way you view and feel about yourself, others, and the world.

As part of a new, courageous Islamic Studies curriculum, *'What is Your Belief?'* aims to help you apply your faith to real-world issues. Features like the *Brain Teaser* boxes and the *Review* and *Reflect* sections show everyday, practical applications of our belief. We pray that this curriculum helps you draw closer to Allah. We would love to improve this curriculum with your suggestions. Please send your feedback to iscurriculum@alhuda.org.

Lastly, we would like to thank Umm Eesaa and Dalia Elamawy for writing these units so beautifully. May Allah accept the effort of everyone who worked on this curriculum, and more importantly, may Allah accept your efforts to get closer to Him.

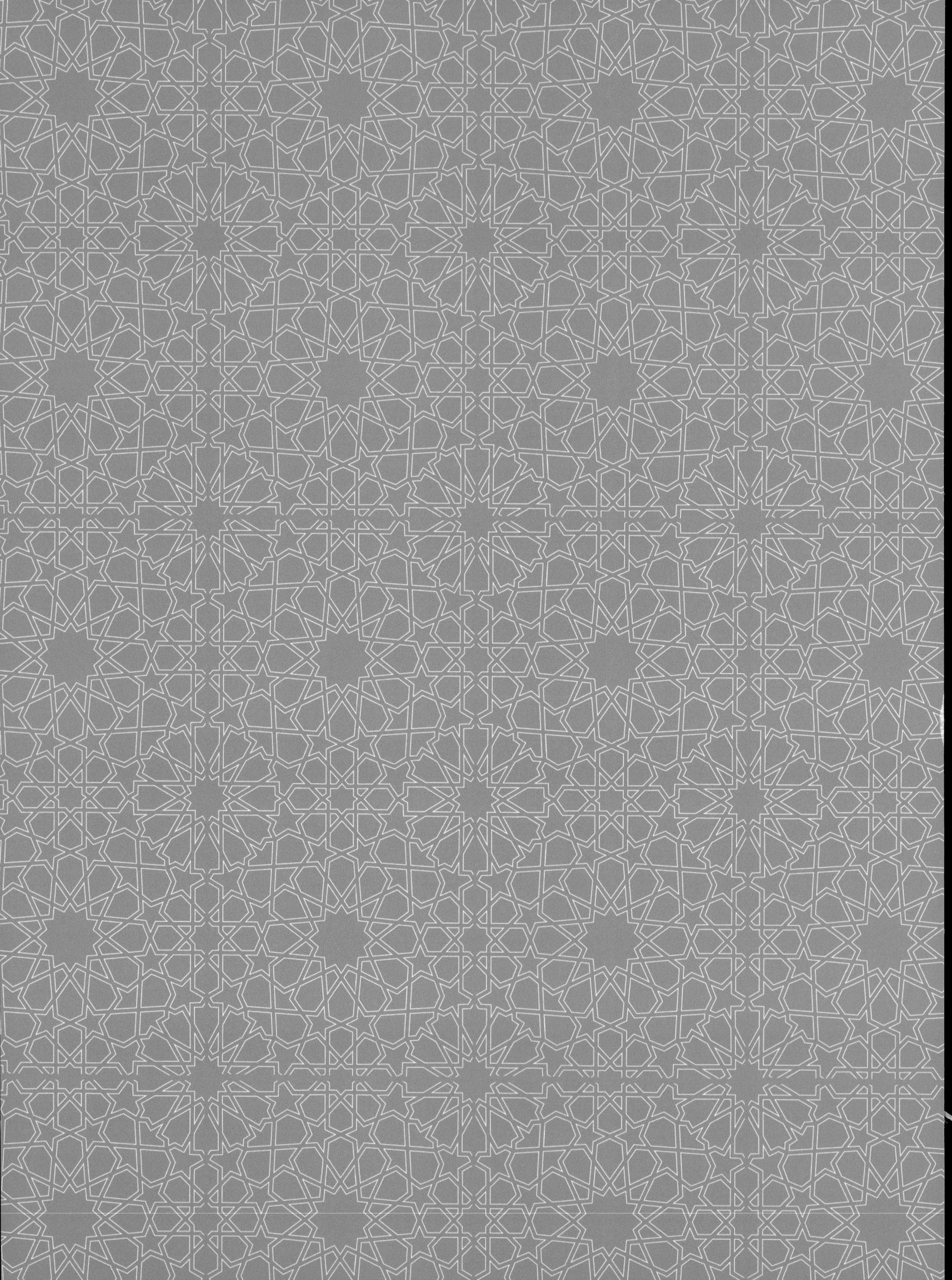

UNIT 1

FINDING PEACE

UNIT 1

Important Vocabulary

Aqada
To tie a knot or to have a contract.

Aqeedah
Term for the Islamic creed and its related set of beliefs.

Belief
Faith in someone or something; acceptance that something exists.

Creed
A set of beliefs. In Islam, it refers to the *shahaadah* (declaration of faith: *La ilaha illa Llah, Muhammadu-rasool Allah*).

Iman
An Islamic term for firm conviction in the heart, leading to affirmation by the tongue and action by the rest of the body. Iman increases and decreases based on the obedience and disobedience to Allah.

Qadar
Divine Decree

TABLE OF CONTENTS

UNIT 1 | FINDING PEACE

Essential Questions

This unit is designed to help answer the following questions.

1. Why do people feel emptiness in their life despite being wealthy?
2. Some say, "I am a good person!" Who decides what is considered good?
3. What is the purpose of our life?
4. How does knowing the correct belief lead to peace in our lives?

CHAPTER 1

EMOTIONAL WELL-BEING

Fatima has been feeling sad lately; she doesn't know why. She feels like she is lacking. She is not pretty enough. She is not smart enough. She does not get enough attention. She is not popular on social media. She notices other girls have their group of friends, yet she feels left out and lonely.

Ahmed was delighted when he got new sneakers. However, that feeling of excitement was short-lived. He saw his friend come to class with nicer sneakers that Ahmed would never be able to afford. Ahmed then felt he wouldn't ever be truly happy until he gets the same or better sneakers. He has an aching emptiness inside him.

Pursuit of Happiness

Though we may seem to have everything we want, we feel a sense of emptiness or sadness. We often don't know why. Sometimes, we try to fill this void by getting more of the things we love. This can include attention from others; for example: *If I were more popular, and I had a certain number of like sand followers, I would be happy*. Or, it may be specific to materialistic desires: *If I had the latest phone, I know I would be happy*. Or sometimes, luxurious goals: *If I go on this vacation, I will be so happy.* You can get those things and feel happy - but only temporarily.

Feeling Void

If a helpless baby was left without a mother at birth, he or she will always feel that something is missing. This will keep nagging them until they are old enough to understand that they did not have a mother. In fact, they would look for another adult figure to fill that void because a mother is a very essential role for a child. In a similar sense, a person who is devoid of Allah in their life and devoid of a clear purpose to their life will feel a constant void.

Filling The Void!

We have both a body and a soul. If we neglect to nurture our bodies, we will have a range of health problems. If we fill our bodies with junk food, we slowly weaken and destroy our bodies. Likewise, if the soul is not nurtured, it will spiritually starve. This void is the sign of a hungry and unhealthy soul begging to be supported.

What is Your Purpose?

No matter how much we try to fill a void with an unhealthy replacement, we will never be able to. Allah created a natural need for Him in all human beings. So our soul seeks this fulfillment. We can fulfill this need by first, learning about our Creator, Allah. And second, by fulfilling the purpose for which we were created: **To worship and revere Allah *alone*** and not to worship ourselves or other people, things or priorities in our lives. To understand life is just not about me, myself, "*my wants, my desires, my dislikes.*" ***Until we understand the true purpose of life, trust the right belief and fulfill what it requires of us,*** we will constantly feel a void in our heart which nothing else can fill.

Finding Peace

The void may increase and manifest in the form of emptiness or depression. Since society does not recognize this need to nurture the soul, people often try to fulfill this yearning in their way, sometimes by yoga, meditation, and spiritual retreats. These various means may relax us and make us happy temporarily. However, the mistake is that we focus on finding happiness as a destination in this world. There is no attention given to any guidance leading to joy in the Hereafter. Upon further reflection, we can see that we don't need to wander to find happiness or to alleviate emptiness. Allah, our Creator, has already informed us how to fulfill our purpose in this life. Only such realization will bring about peace and contentment in our lives. This is the prize sought by most human beings!

Isn't Being a 'Good Person' Enough?

Having an incorrect understanding of the purpose of life leads many to erroneous beliefs.

You may find some saying, *"I am already a good person; I don't need a religion"* or *"I*

believe, as long as no one tells me what to do" or *"I can do as I please as long as I don't hurt anyone."*

You may find it difficult to disagree with someone who states, *"If you are a good person, you should do as you please."* The question now is: Who defines what is *'good'*? What if there are very different opinions about what is good? What appears reasonable to you may not seem so to someone else, i.e., the definition is relative. Everyone may have their own version of good. However, the One who created Good and is the Source of all that is good - Allah - can define good. ***Allah's likes and dislikes define goodness.***

Oftentimes, we may follow the opinions of others and keep up with new trends. We make decisions in life because we believe or we feel it is a right decision. At the same time, unfortunately, we ignore Allah's instructions. Allah is all good and nothing bad comes from Him. Since He has created us, He knows what is best for us. Through revelation, He guides us to what He has determined is good or bad for us. Hence, just because we believe something is good does not make it good. Disregarding Allah's likes and dislikes will not make us good either. On the contrary, this is arrogance that allows us to believe we know better than our Creator.

Some of us claim to love Allah, but we lack motivation when we are called to do good deeds that bring us closer to Him. If we claim to love Allah, then that love should increase our *iman* (firm faith). True *iman* compels us to virtuous deeds. These righteous actions are explained clearly in the *Qur'an* and the *Sunnah*. They help us attain peace and contentment.

SUMMARY

RECIPE FOR HAPPINESS

Islamic belief does not just address happiness in this world, but it presents a recipe for happiness in this world and in the Hereafter - where there is eternal life.

1 CUP OF UNDERSTANDING PURPOSE

TO UNDERSTAND THE PURPOSE OF LIFE IS TO WORSHIP ALLAH

When we know that the purpose of life is to worship Allah, it encourages us to prioritize our life. We then live a purposeful, driven life. It guides us from wandering aimlessly from trend to trend.

1 TSP OF CORRECT KNOWLEDGE

LEARN & UNDERSTAND THE WAY ALLAH WANTS US TO WORSHIP HIM

It is vital to acquire the correct understanding of belief. Acquiring the correct understanding of Islamic belief has an impact on our daily choices. It also leads to developing an unshakable faith (*iman*) within us.

1 DASH OF ACTION

IMAN ENERGIZES US TO WORSHIP ALLAH

It spurs us to act on the knowledge learned. *Iman* propels us to fulfill our responsibility to Allah by doing the things He likes and refrain from things that He doesn't like. This, in turn, creates a sense of contentment, peace and happiness.

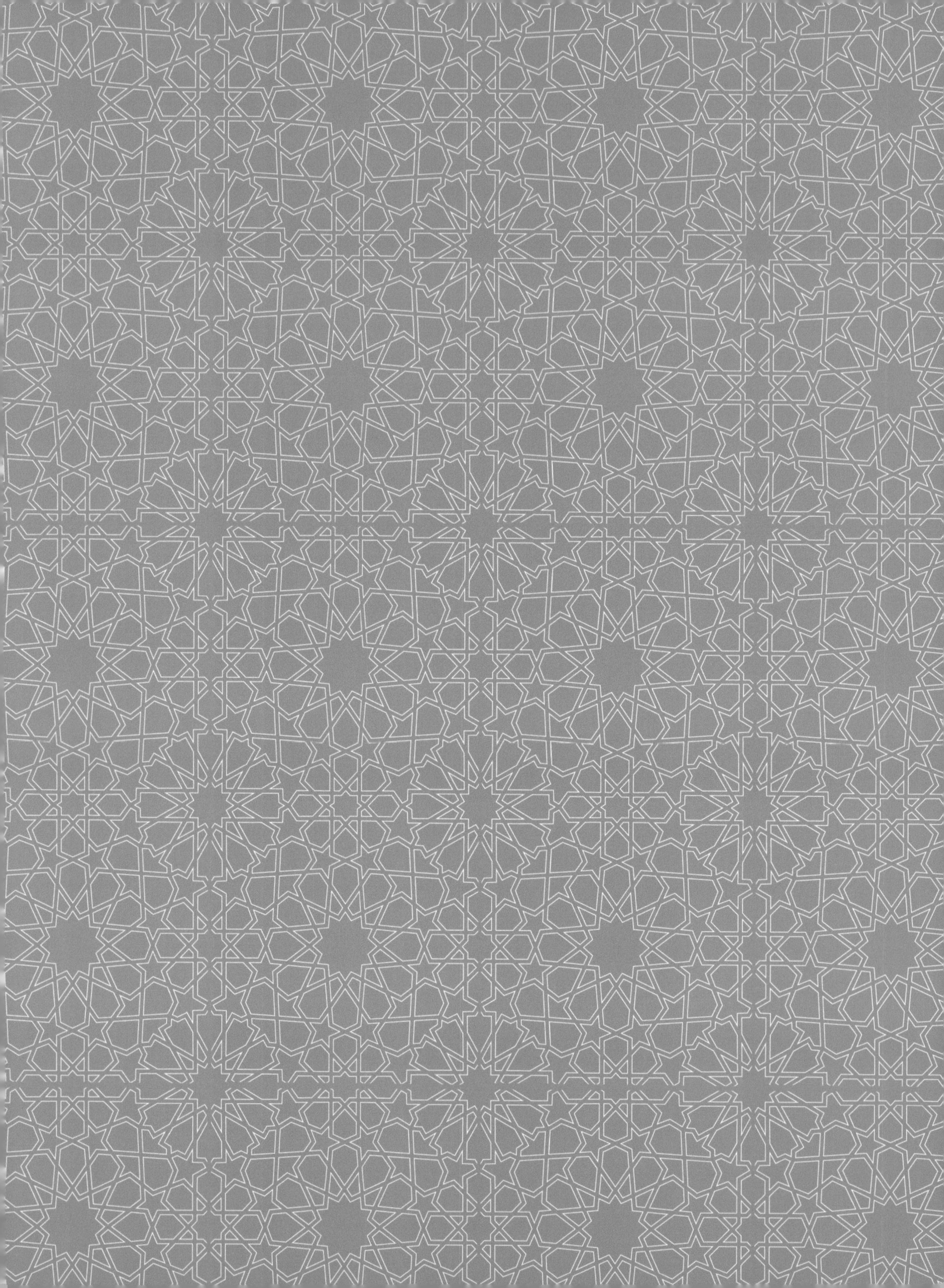

CHAPTER 2

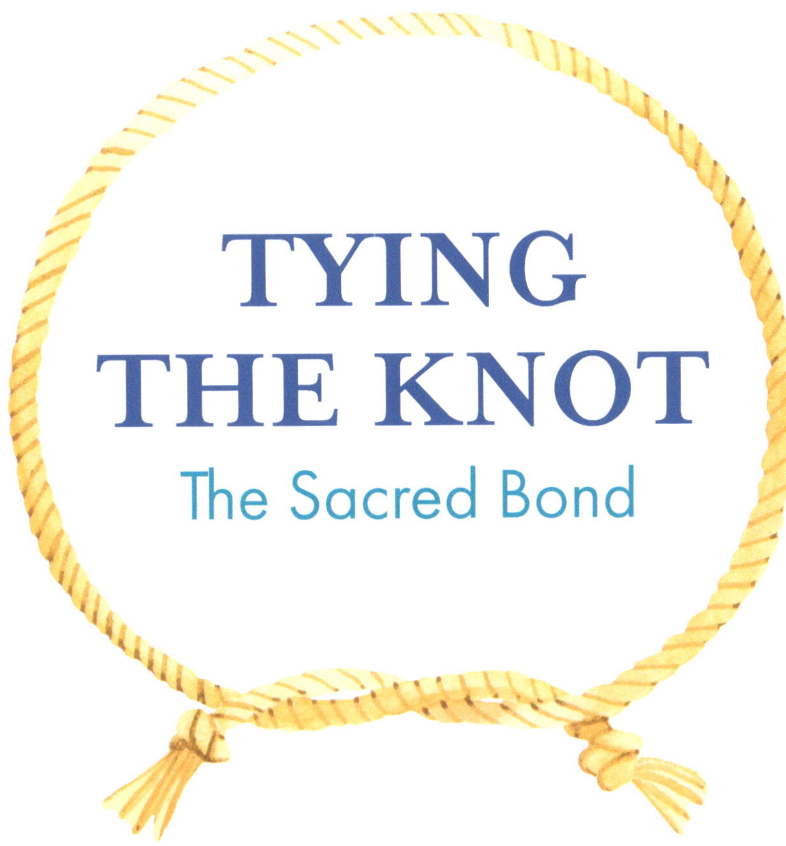

TYING THE KNOT

The Sacred Bond

In Islam, your set of beliefs are called ***Aqeedah.*** *Aqeedah* comes from the Arabic word *aqada* which means to tie a knot. It also means a contract. This word is used to indicate that your belief in Allah is your bond with Him. In other words, it's your contract. It is a pact with Him that you will worship and hold Him as most important in your life. What does it mean to hold *Allah the most important in your life?* It means you value His likes and dislikes above your own likes and dislikes.

What is Belief ?

Every human being believes in something, but what does it mean in Islam? In order for us to understand what it means in Islam, we need to understand two important aspects of Islamic belief.

1. *Aqeedah* (creed) refers to the belief in things which we can and cannot see or did not observe first hand. ***It is not an opinion; it is a belief.***

2. The correct *aqeedah* is the foundation of our entire religion and our entire life. The choices we make in life come with having the correct understanding of our beliefs.

This can be further understood by differentiating facts from opinions.

Beliefs, Facts & Opinions

This difference between facts and opinions can be illustrated by considering the difference between the following two scenarios:

At school, your teacher assigns a heated debate topic: *Should homework be banned in schools?* Your teacher asks you to defend the side that homework should be banned. Your friend has to defend the opinion that homework should not be banned. After researching, you realize that each opinion has strong arguments and research backing it up. Still, you feel your argument is stronger. You start your debate stating, *"I believe that homework should be eliminated or greatly reduced, as it was in Finland."* Is this a belief or an opinion?

Now consider the following scenario. You traveled abroad with your family in the summer, but due to a family emergency, you have to extend your trip. You will not come back in time for the start of school. A close friend calls and informs you that, upon your return, the class has to take an exam that will determine 70% of your final grade. However, when you call another friend, she tells you that there will be no such exam. You decide to believe the first friend, because she is generally more honest and pays better attention to the teacher's instructions. How is this "*belief*" different from that in the previous scenario?

What to Believe?

Well, in the first case, the topic of debate is a matter of opinion. When you say you believe that homework should be banned, what you really mean is that you think it should. Your friend may have another opinion. The opinion is debatable. Both sides may be correct in some ways and incorrect in others. Furthermore, your opinion does not have any serious consequences one way or the other.

In the second scenario, your *"belief"* that there is an exam is very different. It is not a matter of opinion; it is either true or false. There either is an exam or there is not. Both statements cannot be correct. Furthermore, what you believe in this case is important, because it will have serious consequences (your final grade). It will affect your actions and future. If you believe your friend about the exam, you will likely study very hard because your grade depends on it. In other words, you simply cannot afford to believe the wrong thing.

Regarding our religious beliefs, we cannot afford to guess, doubt, or follow whatever is trending in society regarding these beliefs. We cannot afford to be wrong! We need to study and learn to be entirely certain, because everything we do in our lives, as well as our future, depends on it.

Before we learn how to get the correct belief, let's find out how our ideology is constantly being influenced by others, possibly without us realizing it.

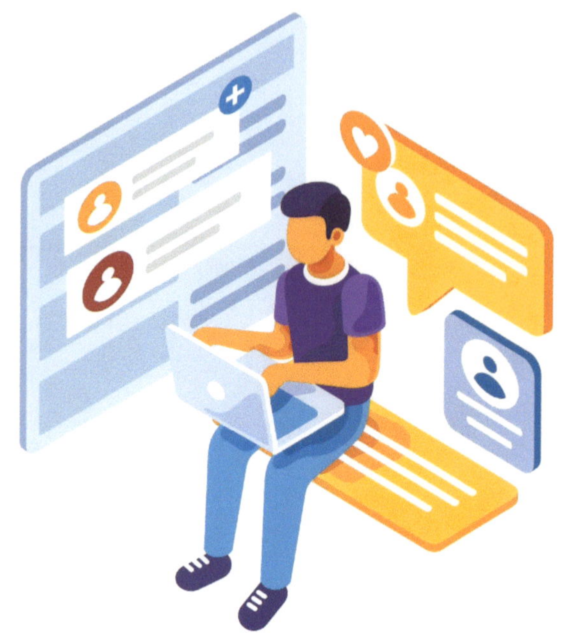

Who is Influencing Your Beliefs?

Imagine that you are watching the news and a tragic crime has occurred somewhere in the world. The criminal has not been identified yet, and as you switch channels, you notice that each news channel is presenting the same facts but with a different twist on it. Each channel has you believing something different, even though the facts haven't changed. Why? Well, people are different and influence others based on their personal biases and opinions. However, where did a fellow human get the authority to have such an impact on what you believe? What makes someone entitled to dictate what others should think or believe? Should we gravitate toward someone's views because they're wealthy or famous, have many followers on social media, or have the most views on their YouTube channel?

In other words, since beliefs are so critical and affect our entire lives, who has the right to tell us what the truth is?

Who Should We Believe?

Who do you think is most qualified to tell us what the truth is? Naturally, it should come from someone who is always truthful. Someone who has complete knowledge of the truth. Someone who has actually witnessed everything that has taken place, so that it is not simply an educated guess. It also has to be someone whose statements are not swayed by emotions, desires, personal motives, or personal experiences. No human being can possibly fulfill these requirements. The ultimate truth can only come from the One who created us and the entire universe, who alone knows the unseen, and knows the realities which He created: Allah. He is the only one who fulfills these requirements. Hence, ***we should take our belief only from Allah since it is based on facts and not opinions.*** Let us explore the benefits of our belief given to us by Allah. Since He is the Most Knowledgeable and Most Wise, only He knows the right belief. Therefore, only He can give us our belief.

Benefits of *Aqeedah* in Our Daily Life

1 IT STABILIZES YOUR THINKING

Prioritizing Allah and His commandments liberates us from other more inferior, stress-inflicting priorities, beings and systems, which constantly torment us and bring us distress and disgrace. Some of us are always worried about who to follow which leads to confusion. Our *aqeedah* brings us peace, satisfaction, clarity and honor. Allah and his Prophet *sallAllahu 'alayhi wa sallam* have compared our belief to a palm tree with deep roots firmly planted in the ground. The tree doesn't bend or fall whenever the winds blow it or whenever anyone shakes it.

2 IT GUIDES YOU

The correct belief illuminates our lives and prevents us from wandering blindly in darkness. It is an internal compass directing you to the best path. In each situation, you will know what decision to make and why. It strengthens you and makes you confident and determined.

How Was Our Belief Communicated?

How did Allah communicate these beliefs to us? Besides the natural *fitrah,* the innate nature He placed in each one of us (this will be discussed in more detail later), Allah out of His mercy also sent us messengers. These Messengers *'alayhumus salaam* are always truthful, knowledgeable, and have witnessed select parts of the unseen. They are not swayed by emotions, desires, personal motives, or personal experiences. Through these messengers, Allah communicates to us. The *Qur'an* is His Speech to us. He also gave the messengers signs to prove that they are really messengers from the Creator. Otherwise, anyone can claim to be a messenger!

We will later offer some evidences proving that Muhammad *sallAllahu 'alayhi wa sallam* was in fact a messenger from God and that the *Qur'an* is indeed the final word of Allah. Let us for now discover the correct belief of a Muslim.

BRAIN TEASER

Imagine you hired a video producer with a contract for their services.

1. Why does this contract require your signature?

2. What happens if this person breaks the contract by not doing a satisfactory job or anything at all?

3. How can this agreement, or any contract in general, relate to our *Aqeedah*?

CHAPTER 2

REVIEW AND REFLECT QUESTIONS

1

Today we see so many rich and famous people struggling in the pursuit of happiness. If you could invite a famous person to Islam what main point would you draw their attention to as to why they haven't found the happiness and peace they long for in their lives?

2

As mentioned in this chapter, Allah's likes and dislikes define what is good and what is not. How do you think you should use this when trying to make decisions in your daily life?

3

Allah has created us and given us free will. He has not left us empty handed in this world but has given us guidance on all aspects of our life. Give two examples on how learning more about your deen helps you find ease in the challenges that you may face on a daily basis?

4

Imagine someone coming to a new city in a foreign country, without any idea of the laws/ fines there. Would it be enough for them to say that they intend on being a good person in order to avoid the consequences of actions that might be wrong under that government? How is this similar to someone saying that being '*a good person*' is enough in their life, rather than following the beliefs and guidelines set by Allah.

5

How does having a strong *aqeedah* help us stay steadfast in our religion?

6

What are the positives in studying Islam under a learned scholar rather than just learning directly from a book in your own bedroom?

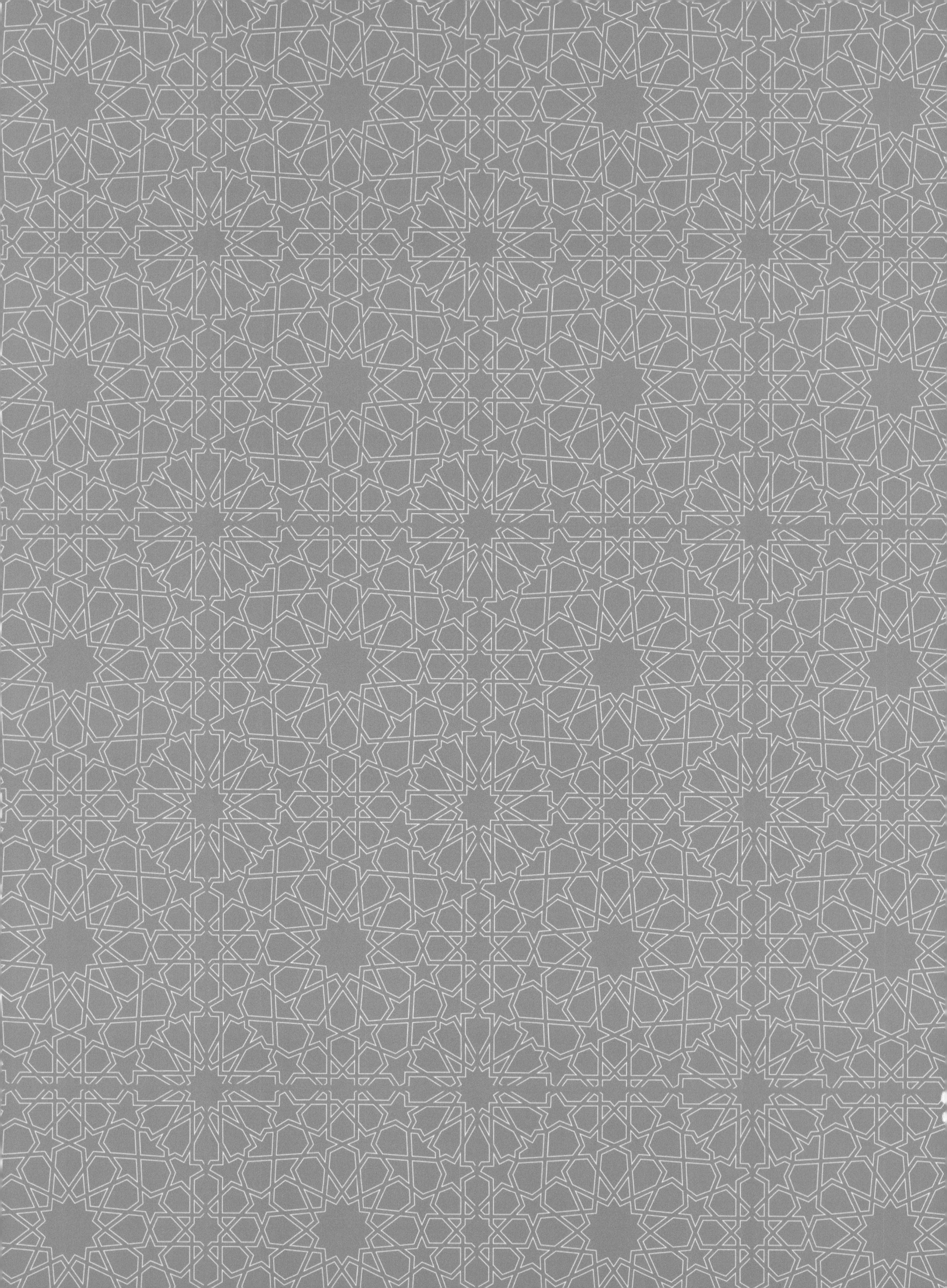

CHAPTER 3

WHAT IS A MUSLIM'S BELIEF?

What is this belief which helps us build a connection with our Creator and grant us eternal happiness? How does it guide us to make right choices in life? The belief of a Muslim, *aqeedah*, is an unshakable, firm belief in the heart which has no doubt in it whatsoever. Once a firm belief is planted inside our hearts, no doubts can shake it. The Islamic *aqeedah* is a set of beliefs brought by the messengers from Allah. It consists of belief in Allah, His angels, His books, His messengers, the Day of Judgment, and Divine Decree. These matters are in the unseen and can only be known by way of revelation from Allah.

PROOF OF BELIEF IN *QUR'AN*

As Allah tells us,

لَّيْسَ ٱلْبِرَّ أَن تُوَلُّوا۟ وُجُوهَكُمْ قِبَلَ ٱلْمَشْرِقِ وَٱلْمَغْرِبِ وَلَـٰكِنَّ ٱلْبِرَّ مَنْ ءَامَنَ بِٱللَّهِ وَٱلْيَوْمِ ٱلْـَٔاخِرِ وَٱلْمَلَـٰٓئِكَةِ وَٱلْكِتَـٰبِ وَٱلنَّبِيِّـۧنَ ...

"Righteousness is not [only] that you turn your faces toward the east or the west, but [true] righteousness is [in] one who believes in Allah, the Last Day, the angels, the Book, and the prophets..." [1]

1. Surah Al-Baqarah [2:177]

PROOF OF BELIEF IN THE SUNNAH OF THE PROPHET, *SALLALLAHU 'ALAYHI WA SALLAM*

When Angel Jibreel *'alayhis salaam* came to the Prophet *sallAllahu 'alayhi wa sallam* in the form of a man and asked him to define belief, the Prophet *sallAllahu 'alayhi wa sallam* responded,

"...that you believe in Allah, His angels, His Books, His Messengers, the Day of Judgment, and to believe in the Divine Decree, be it good and evil." [2]

Hence, Islamic belief is entrenched in proof coming directly from the One who created us. It is not someone's opinion, interpretation or feeling. It is not from a philosopher, a researcher, nor someone on the Internet who has no idea what the purpose of life is. Allah is the only One who could answer these important questions for us: *Why was I created? Where did I come from? What will happen to me after I die?* We cannot be influenced by people who have no knowledge of the basic questions of life. **Can someone who does not know the way, nor has completed the path, guide someone who is lost?**

As mentioned earlier, Allah has already told us the answers to the important questions of life. When we firmly believe in these realities, and abide by their implications, we will live purposeful and fulfilling lives. Only then will our hearts find peace.

2. Sahih Muslim

The Pillars of Belief

All buildings have strong foundations and pillars to hold their weight and prevent them from collapsing. Everything else in the building is built around these pillars that cannot be moved. They are the most important parts of the building. Similarly, Islam has pillars of belief also referred to as the *Articles of Faith* (*iman*). These pillars are the most important aspects of belief, without which our faith would shake and collapse with the slightest disturbance.

THERE ARE 6 PILLARS THAT WE MUST BELIEVE IN:

1. ALLAH
2. HIS ANGELS
3. HIS BOOKS
4. HIS MESSENGERS
5. THE DAY OF JUDGEMENT
6. DIVINE DECREE

BELIEF IN ALLAH

To believe that Allah is the Creator of the Universe, He is the only One Who provides for us. He is our Sustainer and the Sustainer of the entire universe. He is Unique in His names and attributes. He is the only One who deserves to be worshipped.

ALLAH'S ANGELS

Allah has created beings from light. They do not have the ability to disobey Him. Out of His love for us, He has appointed some of them to motivate us to do righteous deeds and others to protect us. We will discuss more about these amazing creations of Allah and their role in our universe.

ALLAH'S BOOKS

Allah has revealed various books over the history of mankind as a form of guidance. Such books include the Scrolls revealed to Ibrahim *'alayhis salaam*, the Torah revealed to Musa *'alayhis salaam*, the Psalms revealed to Dawood *'alayhis salaam*, and the Gospel [Bible] revealed to Isa *'alayhis salaam*. These previous scriptures have been partially or completely lost, and that which remains is not in its original form. The last of the revealed books is the *Qur'an*, which Allah has promised to protect in its original form until the Day of Judgment. We will later discuss more in detail about the preservation of the *Qur'an* and the *Sunnah* of the Prophet *sallAllahu 'alayhi wa sallam.*

ALLAH'S MESSENGERS

Allah has sent messengers from the beginning of time among people to guide them. From Adam *'alayhis salaam* to Muhammed *sallAllahu 'alayhi wa sallam*, He has informed us that the purpose of this life is to worship Allah alone. Through this, we can achieve happiness in this life and in the Hereafter.

DAY OF JUDGEMENT

We are accountable for our actions in this life. We will be asked about everything we did or did not do on the Day of Judgment. Based on our deeds, belief, and the Mercy of Allah, we will enter either Paradise or the Hellfire.

DIVINE DECREE (DESTINY)

Divine decree is the belief that Allah has already written for us what is to come until the Day of Judgment; the good and the bad. Therefore, we do not feel stressed when things are not going our way, nor do we blame others. We recognize and understand that Allah has already decreed this particular situation for us with His Wisdom. Allah knows what path we are going to take, but He does not force us to take that path. If draw closer to Allah and turn to Him in *du'aa*, our destiny can be changed. Therefore, our destiny is coupled with free will. In Unit 2, we will concentrate on the One who knows and loves us most, Allah!

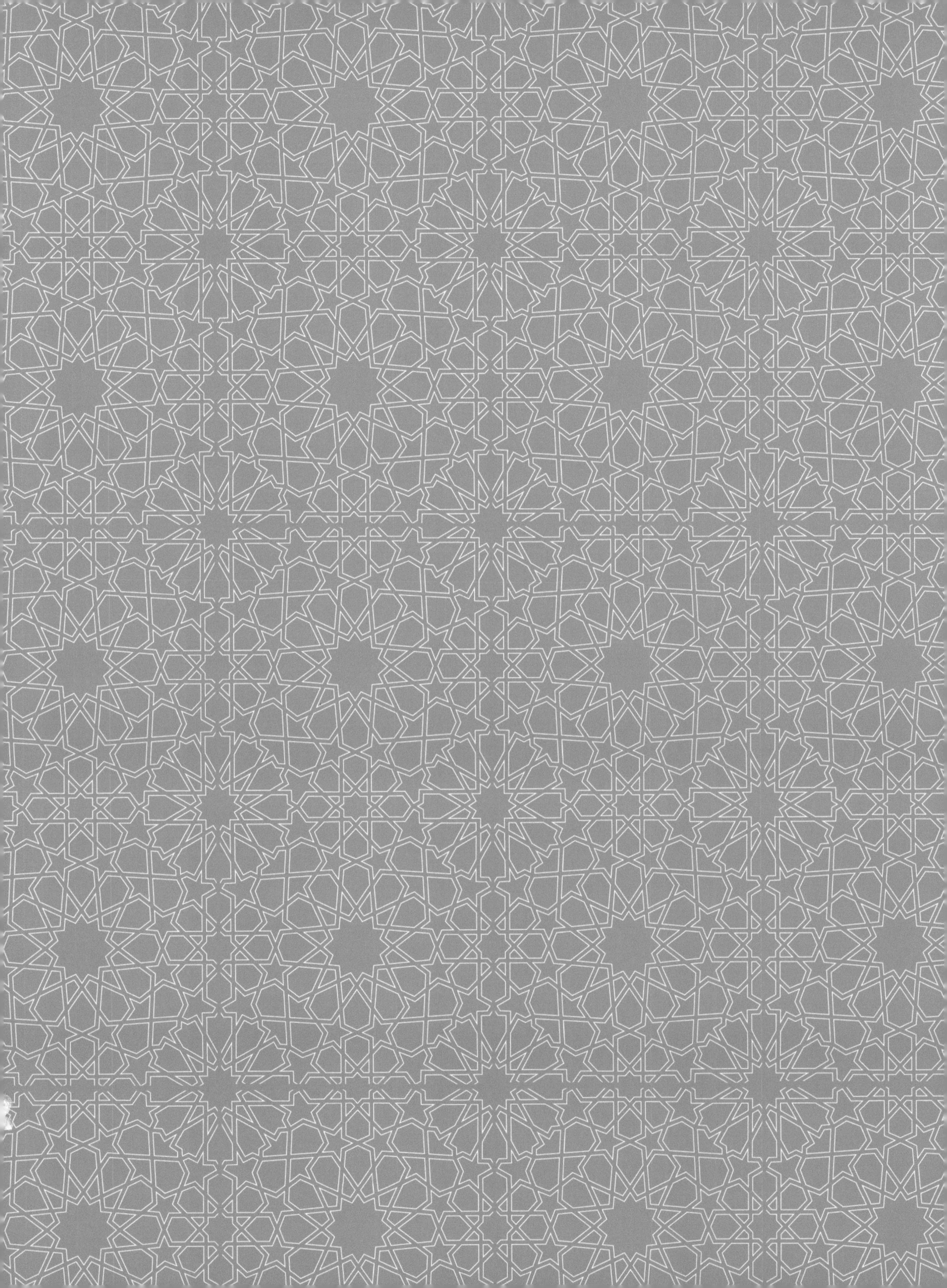

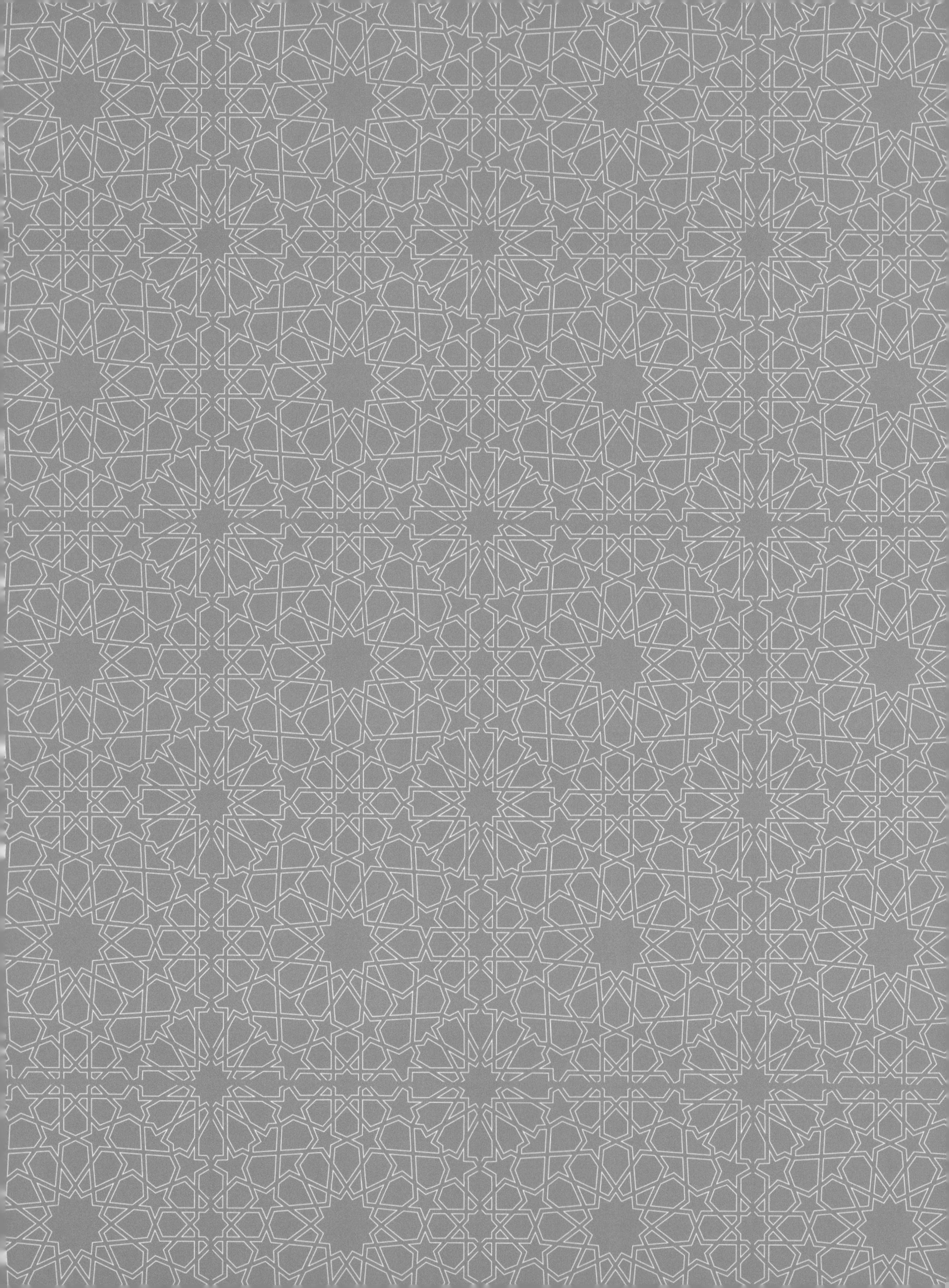

UNIT 2

INTRODUCTION TO OUR CREATOR

UNIT 2

Important Vocabulary

Atheism
Disbelief in an all-powerful God

Belief
Faith in someone or something; acceptance that something exists.

Fardh kifayyah
A communal obligation. An act that must be performed by at least some of the members in the community or all are held accountable.

Fitrah
The *fitrah* is the innate desire to worship Allah alone, instilled in all human beings from birth.

Instinctive
An automatic or unconscious natural instinct.

Monotheism
The belief and worship of one God

Omnipotent
The One who has unlimited power or authority; Allah

Polytheism
The belief and worship of many gods.

Tadabbur
To ponder or reflect on the signs of Allah to draw closer to Him.

TABLE OF CONTENTS

UNIT 2 | BEGINNING TO KNOW OUR CREATOR

Essential Questions

This unit is designed to help answer the following questions.

1. Why do many people turn to prayer in desperate times, regardless of their belief in God?
2. What are the roles of human intellect and revelation in understanding our world?
3. What can we learn about Allah from observing nature?
4. How can science help shape my perception of Allah?
5. Are science and Islam compatible?
6. What does knowing about Allah's perfection mean for me and my life?

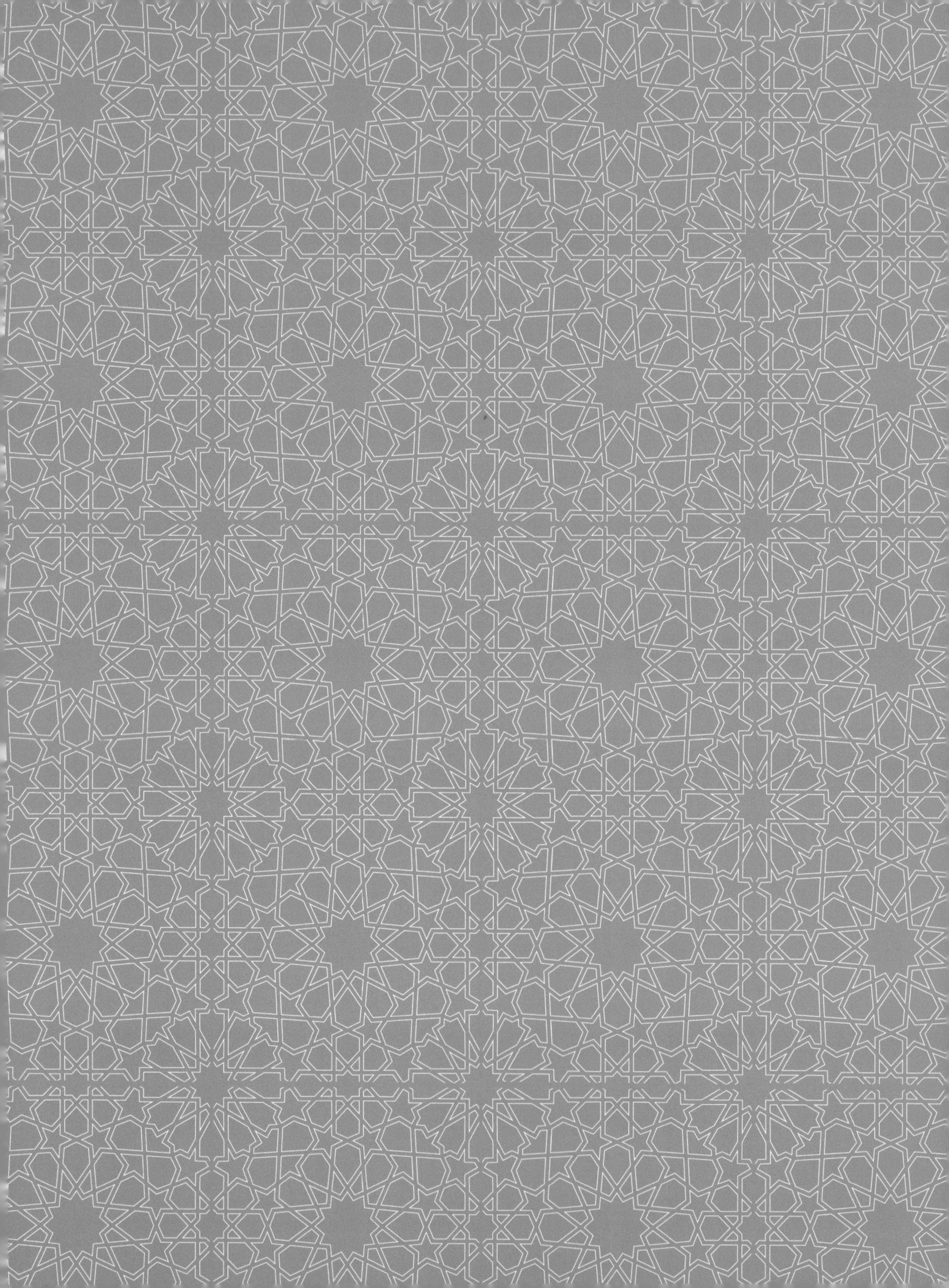

CHAPTER 4

BELIEF IN ALLAH [3]

1ST PILLAR: BELIEF IN ALLAH

We know now that the first and most important principle of *aqeedah* is belief in Allah. All the other pillars depend on this one. With this belief firmly rooted in our hearts, all other beliefs will fall into place. Once we believe in Him and the truth of His revelation, we naturally believe in everything He informed us of [the prophets, the scriptures, the angels, the Day of Judgment, and His divine decree]. Once we have a firm and correct belief in Allah, worshipping and obeying Him becomes natural, easy, and fulfilling. He would then be the One you unconditionally love and revere, as He is the One who brought you into existence and gave you everything you have. He is the One who saved you time and time again from hardship and this will naturally lead to appreciation.

Belief in Allah is the essence of the *Qur'an* and all the revealed scriptures before it. The *Qur'an* describes who Allah is and explains His Names and Characteristics in exceptional detail. Allah explains the fact that He alone is Divine, Perfect, Unique, and Worthy of Worship. Allah proves it in various approaches, including discussions of the signs and wonders of His Creation, logical arguments, descriptions of Himself, responses to common misconceptions, and an account of the history of belief and disbelief throughout time.

---

3. The arguments in this chapter have been primarily adapted from the book *Divine Reality: God, Islam, & the Mirage of Atheism* by Hamza Andreas Tzortsiz.

Allah has given us clear signs and tools by which we can recognize and know Him. We will discuss the tools which Allah has given us to ensure us of His existence.

You Are Pre-Programmed!

EVIDENCE OF GOD BY *FITRAH*: THE NATURAL AND INSTINCTIVE BELIEF

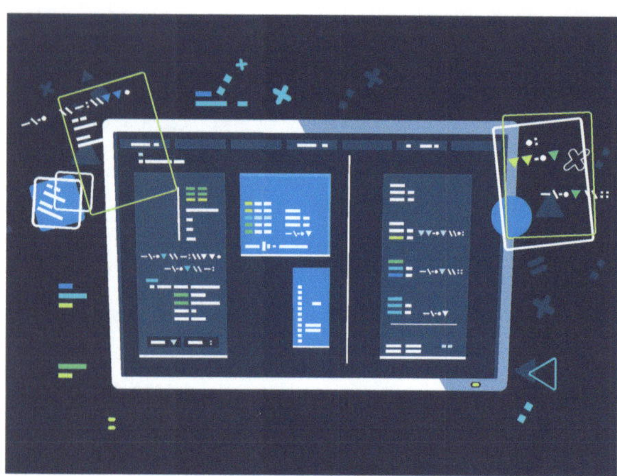

How does a newborn baby know to look for nourishment as soon as it is born? Why are we created with a natural sense of disgust from things that are harmful and unsanitary? Why do we have a natural fear of dangerous creatures? Allah created humans, as well as animals, with natural instincts to help guide their living and protect them in various circumstances. Just as there are physical instincts to guide us, we were also created with psychological and spiritual instincts. Each and every human being was created with a pure nature which intuitively recognizes God. Allah created this natural state within all people to find and recognize the truth. This natural, intuitive belief in a Creator is referred to as ***fitrah*** in Arabic. It is mentioned in the *Qur'an*, in the *hadith* of the Prophet *sallAllahu 'alayhi wa sallam*, and it is discussed in modern science.
Allah said,

فَأَقِمْ وَجْهَكَ لِلدِّينِ حَنِيفًا فِطْرَتَ ٱللَّهِ ٱلَّتِى
فَطَرَ ٱلنَّاسَ عَلَيْهَا لَا تَبْدِيلَ لِخَلْقِ ٱللَّهِ ذَٰلِكَ
ٱلدِّينُ ٱلْقَيِّمُ وَلَـٰكِنَّ أَكْثَرَ ٱلنَّاسِ لَا يَعْلَمُونَ

"So direct your face toward the religion, inclining to truth. [Adhere to] the fitrah of Allah upon which He has created all people. No change should there be in the creation of Allah. That is the correct religion, but most of the people do not have knowledge." [4]

Despite the fact that the *fitrah* is a natural state, it can be covered or spoiled by external influences, from parents or family members to society, social media and peer pressure.

---

4. Surah Ar-Rum [30:30]

The Prophet *sallAllahu 'alayhi wa sallam* explained this saying,

مَا مِنْ مَوْلُودٍ إِلاَّ يُولَدُ عَلَى الْفِطْرَةِ، فَأَبَوَاهُ يُهَوِّدَانِهِ أَوْ يُنَصِّرَانِهِ أَوْ يُمَجِّسَانِهِ، كَمَا تُنْتَجُ الْبَهِيمَةُ بَهِيمَةً جَمْعَاءَ، هَلْ تُحِسُّونَ فِيهَا مِنْ جَدْعَاءَ

"No child is born except on the fitrah, but then it is his parents who make him Jewish, Christian, or Magian (a fire worshipper). (This is) similar to how an animal produces perfect offspring. Do you see any part of its body amputated (naturally when it is born)? " [5]

The *fitrah* includes several aspects, some of which we will discuss below.

Nothing is Greater Than Your Creator

FITRAH: AN INSTINCTIVE BELIEF IN AN OMNIPOTENT CREATOR [6]

A natural and instinctive belief in God, an Omnipotent Creator, is the most significant aspect of the *fitrah*. Not only did Allah and His Messenger *sallAllahu 'alayhi wa sallam* inform us of this, but this is recognized by many psychologists, sociologists, and anthropologists, including some who themselves do not believe in God. In line with the Prophet's *sallAllahu 'alayhi wa sallam* statement about children being born on the *fitrah,* many studies in child psychology have concluded that theism (belief in God) is natural and instinctive to children whereas atheism is not, regardless of whether or not the children are from religious or atheist families. [7]

"A three-year international research project, directed by two academics at the University of Oxford, finds that humans have natural tendencies to believe in gods and an afterlife. The £1.9 million project involved 57 researchers who conducted over 40 separate studies in 20 countries representing a diverse range of cultures." [8]

In conclusion, from His Mercy and Justice, Allah created signs within us that recognize Him as our Creator. This makes it easier on us to follow these instincts, seek the truth, and recognize it as truth once we find it.

---

5. Sahih Al-Bukhari
6. All-Powerful
7. Research Scientist Margaret Evans at University of Michigan Center of Human Growth and Development concludes based on her research that young children favored creationist accounts of the origin of animals over the account of evolution even if their parents or teachers endorsed evolution. Resource: Barrett, Justin L. *"Out of the Mouths of Babes." The Guardian*. (November 2008) https://www.theguardian.com/commentisfree/belief/2008/nov/25/religion-children-god-belief
8. University of Oxford. "Humans 'predisposed' to believe in gods and the afterlife." Science Daily. July 14, 2011. https://www.sciencedaily.com/releases/2011/07/110714103828.htm

"Oh My God"

FITRAH: AN INSTINCTIVE NEED FOR GOD

In life threatening situations, what are the most common things people say? You guessed it! *"Oh God! Save me!"* Allah created us with an intuitive belief in Him, and similarly, He also created within us a natural need to worship Him and call on Him for help. Unfortunately, this natural belief can be corrupted and distorted over time. While some people deny this need to worship God over time, it often reveals itself in times of major distress or desperation. Even people who claim they do not believe in God call on Him or turn to prayer in difficult times.

Allah mentions this in the *Qur'an* in His statement,

وَإِذَا مَسَّ ٱلنَّاسَ ضُرٌّ دَعَوْا۟ رَبَّهُم مُّنِيبِينَ إِلَيْهِ

"And when adversity touches the people, they call upon their Lord, turning in repentance to Him..." [9]

وَإِذَا مَسَّ ٱلْإِنسَـٰنَ ٱلضُّرُّ دَعَانَا لِجَنۢبِهِۦٓ أَوْ قَاعِدًا أَوْ قَآئِمًا فَلَمَّا كَشَفْنَا عَنْهُ ضُرَّهُۥ مَرَّ كَأَن لَّمْ يَدْعُنَآ إِلَىٰ ضُرٍّ مَّسَّهُۥ

"And when affliction touches man, he calls upon Us - lying on his side, sitting or standing; but when We remove his affliction from him, he moves on as if he had never called upon Us regarding the affliction that touched him..." [10]

Here is a heartwarming example: When the daughter of Dr. Lawrence Brown, an ophthalmologist and atheist, was born with a fatal illness, she was taken immediately to the ICU. He found himself in the hospital's prayer room. He stated, *"This was the first time in my life that I felt I had no control and I couldn't do anything about the situation."*

9. Surah Ar-Rum [30:33]
10. Surah Yunis [10:12]

In desperation, he prayed, *"Oh God, if you are there, I need your help! If you save my daughter and show me the correct religion that pleases You, I promise to follow it."* His daughter was miraculously cured as soon as he returned to the hospital room. After thoroughly studying all religions for many years, he eventually became a Muslim and authored several books on comparative religion.[11]

"Non-believers turn to prayer in a crisis, poll finds." The Guardian[12]

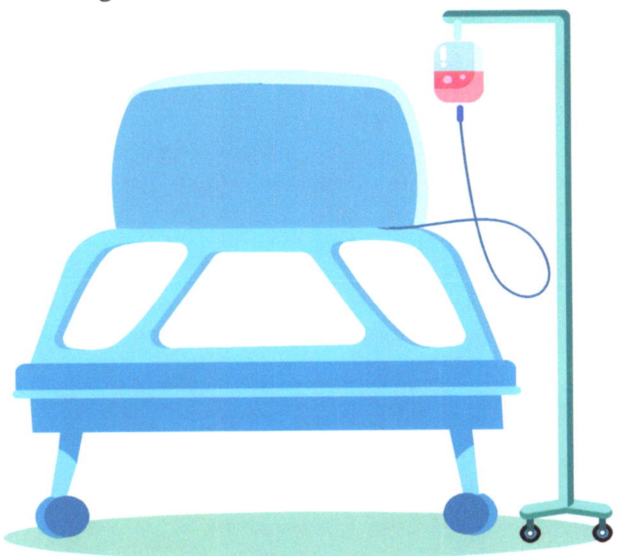

In an article in the Washington Post titled, Some Non-believers Still Find Solace in Prayer, research was cited suggesting that most people, atheists included, naturally turn to God and perform prayer. In several conducted interviews, one conversation with an atheist was highlighted because, in a time of desperation, this individual began a daily *"rigorous prayer routine."* [13]

BRAIN TEASER

Can you identify a non-believer mentioned in the *Qu'ran* who called out to Allah at the very end of his life? Bonus points if you can find which *surah* and *ayaat* is this story mentioned.

11. His full story can be found on several interviews with him on YouTube by searching his name or "Top American Surgeon embraced Islam."
12. Sherwood, Harriet. "Non-believers turn to prayer in crisis, poll finds." The Guardian. January 14, 2018. https://www.theguardian.com/world/2018/jan/14/half-of-non-believers-pray-says-poll
13. Boorstein, Michelle. "Some nonbelievers still find solace in prayer." The Washington Post. January 24, 2013. https://www.washingtonpost.com/local/non-believers-say-their-prayers-to-no-one/2013/06/24/b7c8cf50-d915-11e2-a9f2-42ee3912ae0e_story.html?utm_term=.4429a06dc7b0

Why Are We Here? Discovering Our Purpose

FITRAH: AN INSTINCTIVE BELIEF IN PURPOSE

"I don't know why we are here, but I'm pretty sure it is not in order to enjoy ourselves." [14]

These are the famous words of philosopher Ludwig Wittgenstein. All people, at some point in their lives, ask questions along these lines, *"Why am I here? Is it simply to have fun, eat, drink, make money, have kids, and then die? Then what? How is my life different from that of animals? Where did such a perfectly designed universe come from? If the Creator created this universe with such precision, wouldn't He have a similarly perfect goal for its existence as well as mine? Could it all be simply for nothing in the very end?"*

Where do these nagging questions come from? Why do people experience them? Like the intuitive belief in a divine Creator, this also is a part of the *fitrah* Allah created within us. It is in our very nature to instinctively recognize that we are here for a purpose. Allah created this instinctive belief within us so that we can strive to seek our purpose until we find it.

If you observe everything around you, from the simplest man-made object to the most complex institution, you will find that it all has a purpose: the desk you are working

14. BC Radio, "In Our Time, Greatest Philosopher, Ludwiq Wittgenstein" http://www.bbc.co.uk/radio4/history/inourtime/greatest_philosopher_ludwig_wittgenstein.shtml

on, the clothes you are wearing, the school you attend, etc. Similarly, everything in the natural world has a purpose: your nasal hair, an insect's antennae, the scent of the flower, and the list is endless. Therefore, with the slightest sense of awareness, we realize that **a world designed with this level of complexity and perfection could not have been without purpose.** It would only make sense that spending decades on this earth is for a greater purpose. Would someone put the time and effort to design an educational institution with a sophisticated building, with elaborate equipment and technology, various departments, and a vast library without a reason? Without, for example, allowing anyone to use it nor monetize it? Absolutely not.

How, then, is it possible that this world with all of its complexity is for no official purpose? This is why Allah stated that those who *"reflect on the creation of the skies and earth"* naturally conclude,

"Our Lord, You have not created all of this without purpose - You are far above that!" [15]

ISLAM HAS THE ANSWERS!

Islam has profound answers to these nagging questions that all humans experience. We believe that Allah did not create this natural instinct of purpose for nothing. He wants us to seek our purpose, which in summary is to worship Allah alone. However, worship in Islam is much more

---

15. Surah Ale-Imran [3:191]

than prayers and rituals. It includes all of our daily actions: our character, how we treat one another, small acts and large acts of kindness, our work ethic, our integrity and much more. Worship is pleasing Allah in every act we do, because we love, revere, and obey Him more than anyone else. This not only elevates us, allowing us to reach our full potential, but also liberates us from *"enslaving"* ourselves to society or to others.

All humans have the natural need to worship, devote themselves to, or idolize something or someone in their lives. If we do not worship Allah, we will end up *"worshipping"* other things. This can include friends, social norms and pressures, beauty and fashion, materialism, or even our own selves. A person may, even unknowingly, take any of the above as a *"master"* in that it dictates what a person does and how they should act. However, this will lead to feeling scattered and unhappy, because it is unnatural to worship anything but Allah and

it will not result in the true contentment that our souls desire. The Prophet *sallAllahu 'alayhi wa sallam* expressed this saying,

تَعِسَ عَبْدُ الدِّينَارِ وَالدِّرْهَمِ وَالْقَطِيفَةِ وَالْخَمِيصَةِ

إِنْ أُعْطِيَ رَضِيَ وَإِنْ لَمْ يُعْطَ لَمْ يَرْضَ

"The worshipper of money will be miserable and the worshipper of silk cloaks (i.e. fashion) will be miserable. When he is given (what he wants), he is happy, but when he isn't, he is unhappy." [16]

Similarly, Allah stated,

أَفَرَءَيْتَ مَنِ ٱتَّخَذَ إِلَـٰهَهُۥ هَوَىٰهُ

"Have you seen he who has taken his own desires as his god?" [17]

Allah is One and provides us with one major goal and purpose. Therefore, it places our hearts at ease. When our hearts are at ease, the possibilities are endless. He knows what will make us achieve our highest potential in the short time we are on earth.

16. Sahih Al-Bukhari
17. Surah Al-Jathiyah [45:23]

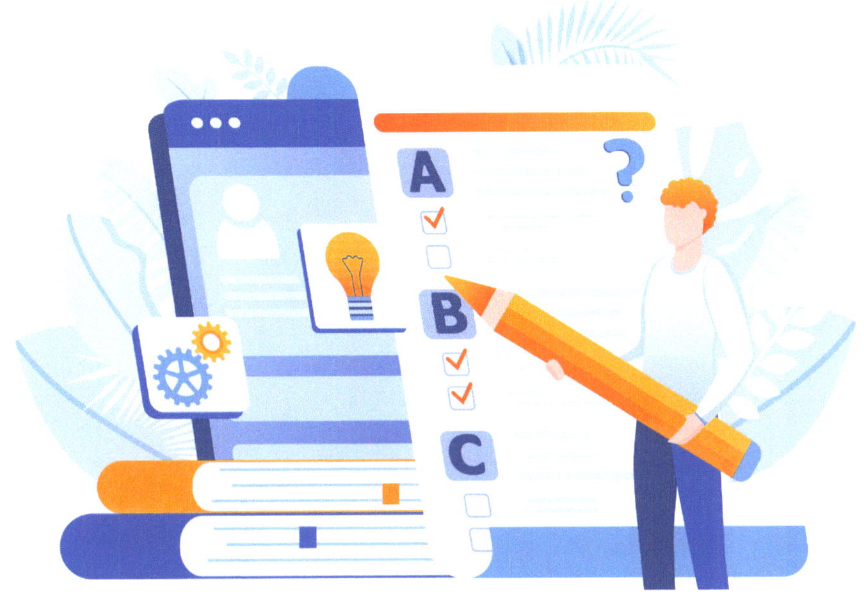

CHAPTER 4

REVIEW AND REFLECT QUESTIONS

1

How do we know who or what to believe? What are the characteristics that need to be present in order to consider any information as true facts?

2

Stop and think about who has the most influence on you in today's world? Give three reasons on why this may be problematic?

3

How does believing in the Day of Judgement help make our life more purposeful?

4

Islam is a way of life, and that means that everything we do from how we go to the bathroom, to how we eat, and how we talk are all guided by the *Qur'an* and *Sunnah*. What will happen when we put our focus on Allah first in all that we do?

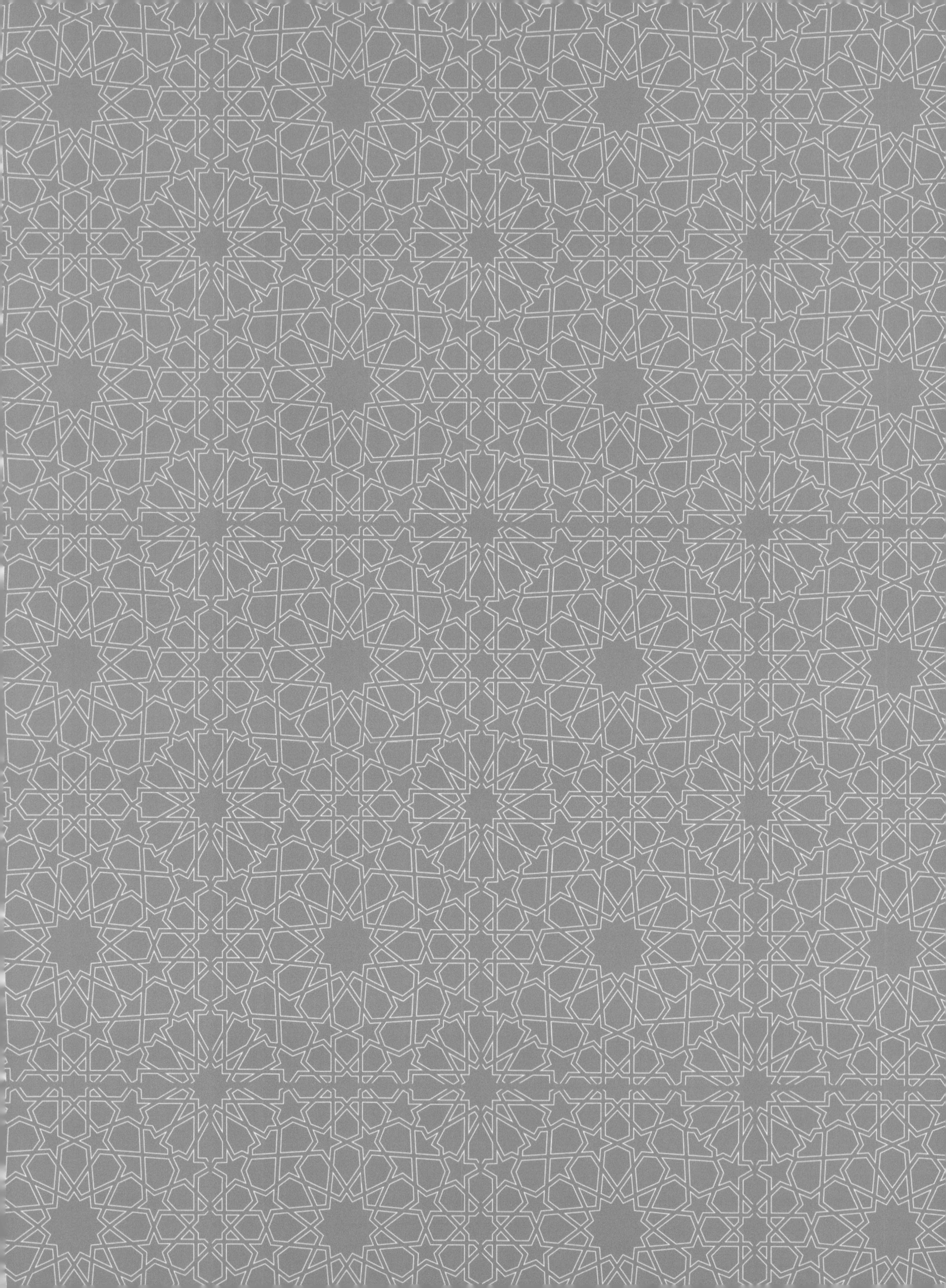

CHAPTER 5

EVIDENCE OF ALLAH'S EXISTENCE

Have you ever asked yourself why the Earth doesn't just spin off its orbit, sending everything on it flying into space? Or how incredible each of the cells in your body functions to keep you alive and healthy? Indeed, it is the force of gravity that keeps the Earth in orbit of the sun, and pulls everything on the surface of the Earth towards the center. You would also find out about the role of ribosomes, or the nucleus' role as the powerhouse of the cell. But is there more to these wondrous creations? Is it just an accidental force that, somehow, keeps everything in order, or does the incredible complexity of it point to the fact that there is *intelligent design?* That there is a Creator who causes and governs all of these things? Should we accept the idea that it all happened randomly, without any purpose? Islam offers us an intuitive framework to understand the physical world that Allah has created. Let us explore beliefs of those who don't acknowledge Allah as a Creator.

What is Atheism?

Atheism is an ideology that centers around the disbelief in the existence of God. There are those who actively claim there is no God, while others who passively say there is no proof of the existence of God.

Let us explore the atheist belief that there is no God. We would be left with no explanation for the absolutely staggering design of the universe itself - from the complexity of the microscopic and the vast alike, to the absolute perfection of their design. The *Qur'an* asks a very relevant question in this regard:

أَمْ خُلِقُوا۟ مِنْ غَيْرِ شَىْءٍ أَمْ هُمُ ٱلْخَـٰلِقُونَ

أَمْ خَلَقُوا۟ ٱلسَّمَـٰوَٰتِ وَٱلْأَرْضَ بَل لَّا يُوقِنُونَ

"Or were they created by nothing? Or were they the creators [of themselves]? Or did they create the heavens and Earth? Rather, they are not certain." [18]

Humans are the most intelligent creatures that exist in the known universe. Yet, humans are unable to create even a fly, let alone themselves or the heavens and Earth! So what can we make of the idea that somehow, all of the creation came about by chance with no indication of a Creator?

What is Deism?

Another ideology which is prevalent today society is Deism. Deism is the belief that God exists and created the world, but beyond that, God has no active engagement in the world except the creation of human reason. Deists were very influential in Great Britain, France, Germany, and colonial America in the 17th and 18th centuries. They were impatient with the denominational wars in Europe; and deism became a religious position associated with reason and the Enlightenment. Freemasons openly embraced deism, as did Unitarians. The pyramid pictured on the obverse of the U.S. dollar bill depicts the all-seeing eye of the deistic God.

Can thoughtful Muslims be deists? Deists affirm that God creates the world from nothing, as mentioned in the Qu'ran. Yet, deism presents a problem. The God of Moses and Jesus and Muhammad may peace be upon them all, Allah, is an active God, one who is immanent and involved in the ins and outs of our lives. One who

---

18. Surah At-Toor [52:35-36]

controls earthquakes, tsunamis, hurricanes and hears the cries of His servants and answers their prayers in everyday life.

What is Agnosticism?

It is a view that justifies not following a religion because they believe they can't intellectually comprehend God's existence. Therefore, they neither believe nor deny God's existence. Can one use their limited intellect to make a call on the existence of God? Let us find out what is the proper way to use our God-given intellect to recognize and affirm His existence.

What is The Proper Use of Our Intellect?

Our complex intellect is what sets us apart from the insects, frogs, whales, and apes. Allah has equipped us with all the tools, including the intellect, needed to fulfill our purpose of worshipping Him.

Let us use a simple analogy to understand how the human intellect is a tool given to us by Allah. As is the case with any tool, only when you use it properly, will it achieve the purpose for which it is intended. Imagine that you are building a marvelous skyscraper and are given the material to do so. However, the only tool at your disposal is a chainsaw.

You would soon find that the chainsaw cannot do the job alone, it will need other tools to assist. If you insisted on using it alone, it would only destroy the great feat you aim to achieve. Similarly, if you give your intellect unconditional authority without anything else, it would only lead to destruction. If you were to attempt to disprove the existence of Allah, then you are using your intellect exactly like the chainsaw - as a tool of destruction, obliterating anything meaningful you wish to achieve with it. Allah describes those who disbelieve in Him as lacking reason to the degree that they are more astray than cattle:

أَمْ تَحْسَبُ أَنَّ أَكْثَرَهُمْ يَسْمَعُونَ أَوْ يَعْقِلُونَ
إِنْ هُمْ إِلَّا كَالْأَنْعَامِ ۖ بَلْ هُمْ أَضَلُّ سَبِيلًا

"Or do you think that most of them hear or reason? They are not, except like cattle. Rather, they are [even] more astray in their way." [19]

Many ideologies prevalent in society are a reflection of an improper use of our intellect. Our intellect is limited and can only process things based on what our senses can see or feel. It cannot fathom things which are unseen and not felt by our senses. That is where we depend on authentic revelation from Allah to learn about things which are unseen. The authentic revelation then supersedes our intellect and it guides our intellect to understand the unseen as mentioned in the revelation. Many people have faltered and gone astray when they try to give precedence to their intellect over the revelation. As Muslims, we recognize and understand the limitation of our intellect and rely on the revelation from Allah in matters of belief and the unseen. ***We give Allah's revelation precedence over our own intellect.***

Science Has Limits

You know that there is more to you than just flesh and blood. What do we say of the human soul? What makes the collection of cells in our bodies different from that of say, a magnolia tree? If you were to take a section of tissue from your heart and a section from the bark of the magnolia tree, and compare them under a microscope, you would find them to be quite similar in structure and composition. However, what if someone were to use that observation to conclude that your heart is ultimately

19. Surah Al-Furqan [25:44]

no different from the bark of a tree? Both are made of cellular matter, and both will die then cease to exist in any way. It could be argued that since this is all that we can perceive with our senses, it is all that we can affirm. How would you respond? Perhaps you would point to the indisputable awareness of complex feelings and drives that you feel in the lump of muscle tissue that is your heart - essentially, of a soul. Yet, you would be unable to prove it through science alone.

Science Can't Explain it All

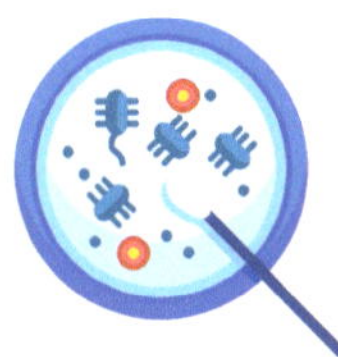

Since science derives understanding based on our senses. Things have to be heard, touched, tasted, seen or smelt. It can't explain processes and phenomena which can't be measured by anything other than these senses. This is where the proper belief in Allah, beginning with our *fitrah* [20], is crucial- because ultimately, science can only take us so far in our understanding of the world. For example, can we scientifically prove that love exists? Can we scientifically observe justice or equality? These are abstract ideas that exist beyond the perimeter of the scientific sphere. Once we try to understand things that are abstract or beyond the natural world [i.e. supernatural], such as the soul, science just doesn't do the job. This is the point - it is simply never going to be enough to give us a complete picture of the life of this world and beyond.

The truth is, **current forms of atheism actually take science as their governing worldview, or religion**, where complex realities must **only** be explained by material causes. To them, everything else is just fiction or superstition. But let's take a step back and challenge the premise: What right does anyone have to say that the scientific process is all we need to understand the world, and that belief in God is doubtful? After all, it is just - a process- one that even the most knowledgeable in its fields will admit has its flaws and limitations. Science itself is not free from bias, nor can it explain anything beyond what can be perceived by the five senses. It is a well-known principle in the scientific community that science cannot disprove the existence of God. In fact, there is a movement among some of the scientists who realize that there is a Creator to this intelligent design.

---

20. As discussed in the previous chapter, *fitrah* is the innate desire to worship Allah alone, instilled in all human beings from birth.

Lamya and The Atheist

Consider this, an atheist approaches a *da'wah* table that regularly sets up weekly at a local university campus and claims that he cannot believe in God or the afterlife because it is not observable by anyone living. One of the bright young Muslim students, Lamya, who happens to be studying Biology, has had her faith questioned before by other students in her class, and even by her own professors at times. She's thought carefully about how to answer these questions and responds by stating that before the invention of the electron microscope in 1931, observing atoms was impossible. Does this mean that atoms did not exist until 1931 when we could see them? Certainly not! It means that we did not have the capability of observing the atoms before that time. Similarly, she says, *"We do not have the capability of seeing Allah or the afterlife until after death. Even still, we are surrounded by countless signs in the world around us that point to the existence of a Creator. Indeed, the real test lies in believing in Him and the afterlife without seeing them directly."* The proof of Allah's existence is literally everywhere- within ourselves and in everything around us. Truthfully, we do not need to go to great lengths to refute those who deny it, because the evidence of a Creator is as clear as the sun in a cloudless sky.

"No matter what scientific evidence is amassed to explain the architecture of atoms, or the ways that neurons exchange chemical and electrical signals to create the sensations in our minds, or the manner in which the universe may have been born out of the quantum foam, science cannot disprove the existence of God — any more than a fish can disprove the existence of trees."

— Alan Lightman. [21]

21. Alan Lightman is a physicist and professor at MIT says, taken from book review: "Why Science Does Not Disprove God." by Amir D. Aczel - The Washington Post

Islam & Science Can They Get Along?

It's important to know that Islam does not demand that we denounce science. Rather, we are encouraged and, at times, required to study it and become proficient in its various branches as a *fardh kifaayah.* [22]

A Muslim's faith is strengthened by knowing how the world functions, and by innovating new ways and technologies to benefit mankind. We should always try to use the tools Allah has given us to strengthen our belief.

In reality, the proofs of nature fit very comfortably in the embrace of Islamic proofs of Allah. When we understand that science is not at odds with the *Qur'an* and is in fact a tool given to us by Allah to make sense of our world, we are able to use our understanding of the world to give us the right momentum to worship Him eagerly. The Islamic frame of mind offers us the ability to perceive the world around us as compelling signs of Allah's power. Thus, in history, we see that the scholars who were well-versed in Islamic knowledge simultaneously had a deep drive to excel in the knowledge of worldly matters, because doing so would improve their worship of

BRAIN TEASER

What is one evidence that always reminds you of Allah - the One and only Creator? Why?

22. *Fardh kifaayah* refers to the communal obligation that should be fulfilled by at least some members of the ummah.

the Creator. In fact, in a time when Europe was hobbling through its Dark Ages, crippled by social, moral, and intellectual stagnation after the fall of the Roman Empire, the Islamic Empire ushered in the new world with its Golden Age of knowledge and innovation which spanned from the 8th to the 14th centuries CE.

Huda's Discovery!

Huda is a young lady who has always been fascinated by history, but also had a sense that the history she's been taught in school was somewhat biased. She found that there was very little mention of the Islamic contributions to the world, and if there was, it was usually portrayed in a negative light or at best, neutrally. During her summer break, she decides to research more about the Golden Age of Islam that was briefly mentioned in school and discovers that during this era, the Islamic empire was burgeoning with scholars progressing leaps and bounds with advancements in medicine, astronomy, physics, chemistry, and literature, among other sciences. She learns that the entire mathematical field of Algebra is actually named after the book written by the famous Muslim scholar

Muhammad Ibn Musa Al-Khwarizmi, called *Kitab Al-Jabr.*

"...Islamic scholars invented decimal fractions and trigonometry adapted to astronomy and cartography. Mathematical models of the heavens from Islamic observatories fueled Copernicus's discoveries, and Ibn Sina [edited by author to use original name rather than Latinized name of Avicenna] 10th-century Canon of Medicine became the basis of Western medical study for the next 700 years. The astrolabe, an analog computational device used in astronomy in the Islamic world, shaped the future of navigation, allowing sailors to determine their latitude" [23]

— Andrew T. Bay

Interestingly, these Islamic scholars who spent their lives studying the *Qur'an, Hadith, Fiqh,* and other Islamic disciplines, also bore the torch that led the world in scientific advancement, because they were deeply driven to worship Allah. It was their desire to truly glorify and exalt Allah that pushed them to innovate in ways to better serve Him and humanity at large.

Can you think of other inventions that help us to better serve Allah and/or humanity? Explain.

For example, the astrolabe is a highly-sophisticated computing device that is considered the predecessor of both the digital computer and the telescope. But did you know that its development was due in large part to the need for calculating times for prayer as well as direction to *Qiblah*? In Islam, we are constantly encouraged to try to be the best of both worlds - the world of this life, and the world of the hereafter.

23. Islamic Renaissance Man by Andrew T. Bay (BA '91, MA '94) in BYU Magazine Summer 2017

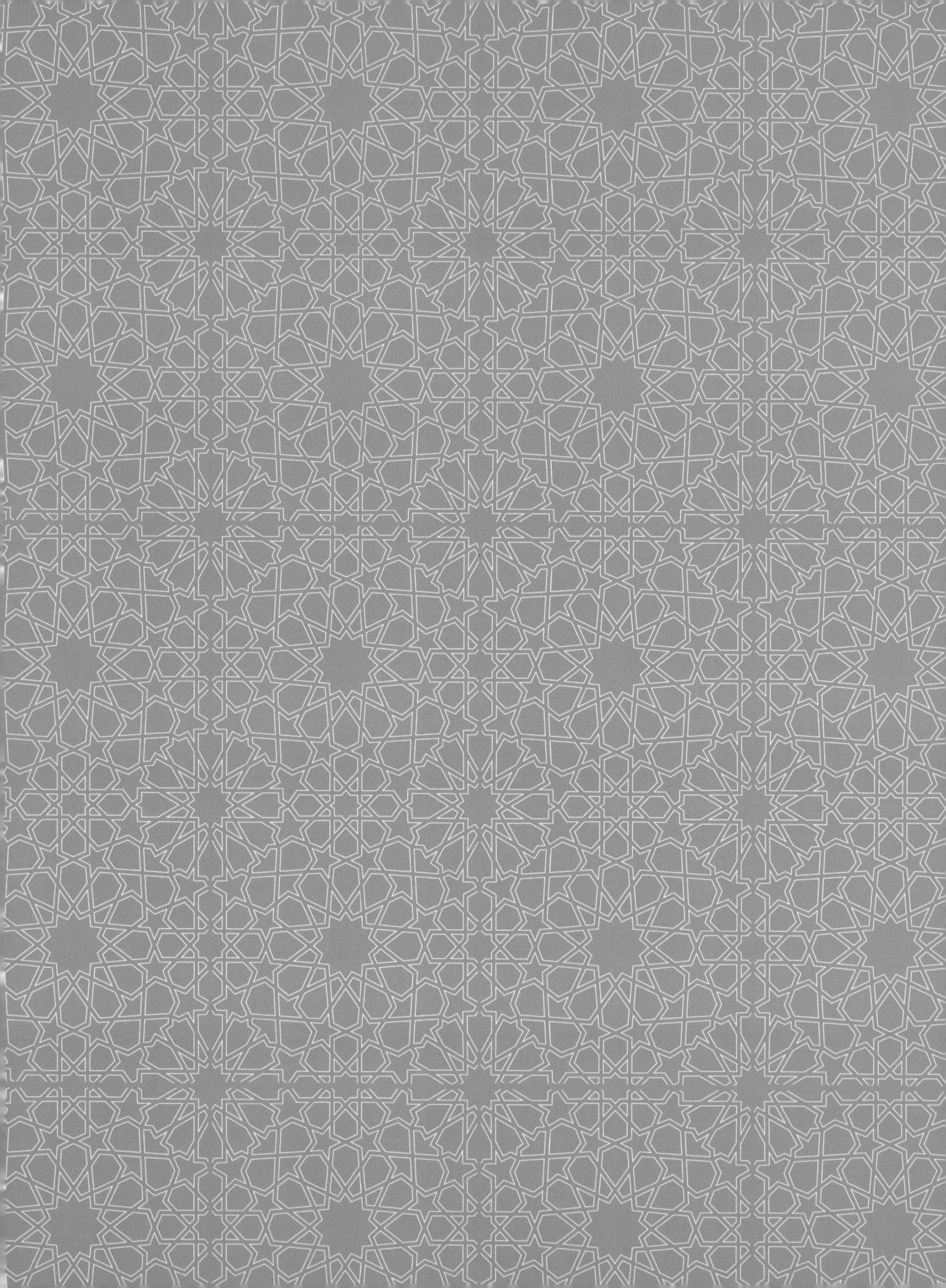

 CHAPTER 6

THE DESIGN OF THE UNIVERSE

IS IT MOTHER NATURE?

Let us begin with a short exercise: Think of just one object from the natural world and make a short list of everything you know about it. How does it look? How does it function? Where does it exist? What natural processes led to its formation? If you study your object long enough, you would likely find yourself filled with wonder and amazement at its perfect design and function.

Now, imagine that someone comes along and claims that the marvel you have just studied has actually come about by chance. Or that an ambiguous, undefined force called Mother Nature [24] has caused it without any intention or intelligence behind it. In truth, the term Mother Nature has gained traction in mainstream thought largely due the growth of secularism and atheism, when referring to any event or creation of nature. For example, it is

24. The origins of the term *Mother Nature* has its roots in Greek mythology from the belief in Mother Gaia, a goddess who personifies nature and is considered to the source and guiding force of creation.- **Merriam Webster Dictionary**

common to hear something like: *"Mother Nature has given us the relief of rain after a long drought!"* It has also become common to credit the universe with things that are not in its control, such as saying *"The test was postponed to tomorrow because my teacher came late... Thank you universe for the extra day to study!"* What is more curious, is that no one even thinks twice upon hearing this.

Living in a post-religious society [25] comes with its challenges- it sometimes means that those who try to hold fast to their Islamic belief find themselves pressured to shy away from even mentioning God in their everyday speech. It has become socially frowned upon to discuss God or religion in a public school setting or in the workplace, and we may at times feel pressured to just go with the flow, so to speak. Have you ever found yourself or someone you know crediting Mother Nature, the universe, or its variant (i.e. nature, the *"force,"* etc.) with something that only Allah could have done? If so, understand that this idea is not new and it is a carefully crafted shroud made to cover and, eventually, blot out all notions of God altogether. Allah tells us,

وَقَالُوا۟ مَا هِىَ إِلَّا حَيَاتُنَا ٱلدُّنْيَا نَمُوتُ وَنَحْيَا
وَمَا يُهْلِكُنَآ إِلَّا ٱلدَّهْرُ وَمَا لَهُم بِذَٰلِكَ مِنْ عِلْمٍ
إِنْ هُمْ إِلَّا يَظُنُّونَ

"And they say 'There is nothing beyond our worldly life. We die; others are born. And nothing destroys us but the passage of time.' Yet they have no knowledge in support of this claim. They only speculate." [26]

The universe does not just make things happen randomly, nor did it come into existence randomly. When you begin to examine the theories of design-by-chance or design-by-undefined force of nature, it doesn't take much to uncover their faults. The major flaw underpinning these theories is that though they may explain how nature operates, they fail to answer essential questions, such as, who or what originated the universe and its contents to begin with? Who or what governs the forces of the universe and keeps them from

25. Post-religious means that the society no longer has any religion as the dominant influence of norms and morals.
26. Surah Al-Jathiyah [45:24]

erupting into chaos? Only when confronted with a question that undeniably points to the existence of a Creator, would their adherents say, *"This is something unknown."*

As Muslims we refrain from saying such false phrases like *"the universe"* or *"Mother Nature"* did such-and-such, even when our intentions are not to deny Allah. We should instead be fully conscious of our speech, knowing that one day, we will be held accountable for it. If you make a meaningful effort to align your speech with that which pleases Allah because you know that it is ultimately only He who matters, you are already fortifying your own faith and beginning to sow the seeds of *da'wah* [27] to those who have doubts or who deny Allah altogether.

The Universe Must Have a Creator

So, what caused the universe to exist? The idea that all of it - the beginning, the order that came in it, the perfect design and function- happened by accident, is one that is unconditionally impossible. What would happen if you randomly attempted to achieve such order with a much more complex system? The probability is so small that practically speaking, it reaches a level of impossibility. For just a **single cell** to be made, it entails the perfect arrangement of trillions of molecules into proteins, nucleic acids, sugars and fats that then become different working parts. It's safe to say that claiming it happened by chance defies all sound logic. What, then, of the perfect equilibrium we find in the entire universe?

27. *Da'wah* is a broad term which means *"inviting to the worship of Allah,"* and has many avenues.

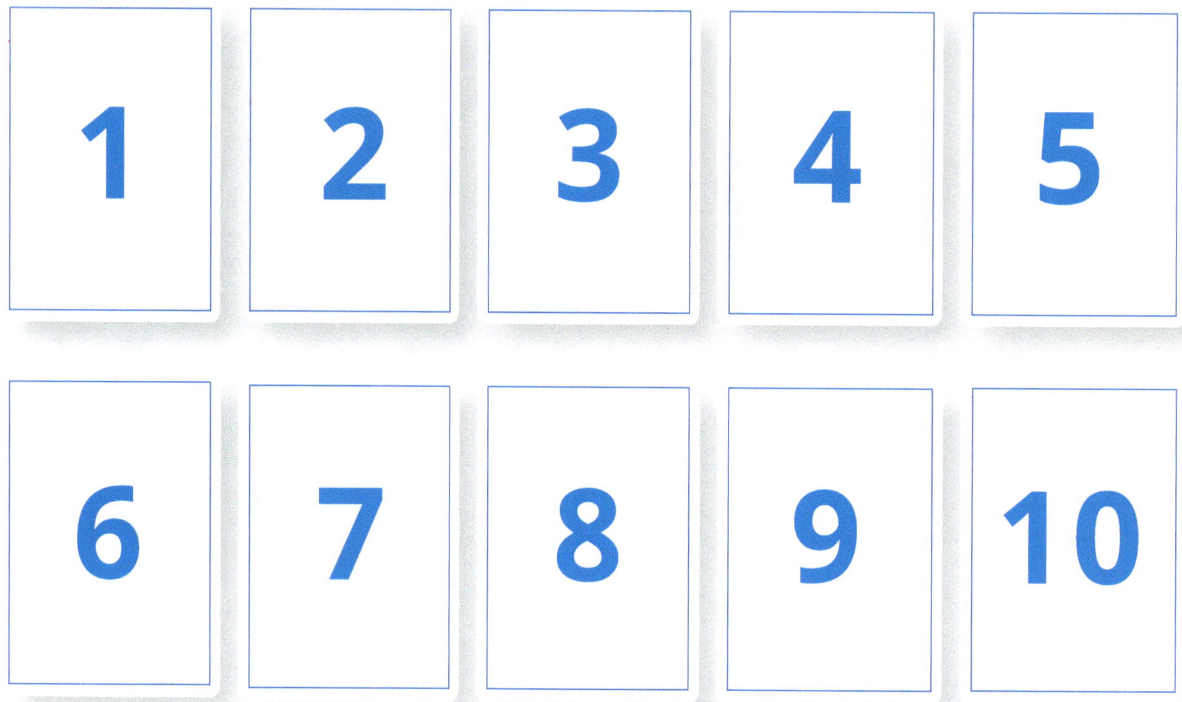

Take ten blank flash cards and number them from one to ten. Then, shuffle them and place them in your pocket or in a box. Without looking, draw one card out after another until you've taken out all ten. Did you take them out in numerical order, from one to ten? The probability that you've done so is 1 in 3,628,800; and this is only for an ordered arrangement of one to ten!

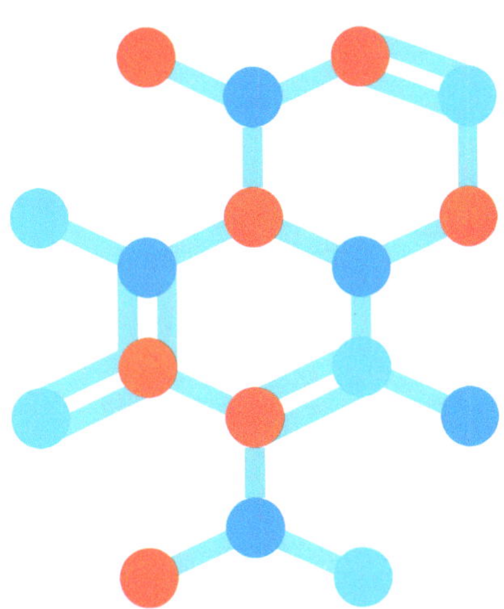

Making a Meaningful Connection

Ponder the marvel of creation - see how beautifully it is all put together, how it all works so perfectly - it will no doubt evoke in you a deep appreciation and awe for Allah, your Creator. Allah says:

وَسَخَّرَ لَكُم مَّا فِى ٱلسَّمَـٰوَٰتِ وَمَا فِى ٱلْأَرْضِ
جَمِيعًا مِّنْهُ إِنَّ فِى ذَٰلِكَ لَـَٔايَـٰتٍ لِّقَوْمٍ يَتَفَكَّرُونَ

"And He has subjected to you whatever is in the heavens and whatever is on the earth - all from Him. Indeed in that are signs for a people who give thought." [28]

From the complexity of the microscopic, to the magnificence of the cosmic; from the elegance of forces working together in perfect harmony, to their oftentimes catastrophic nature--all of the beauty and power we see in this universe point to the action of a single omniscient, omnipotent Creator. Isn't it truly humbling to know that the Creator, Allah, has created all of this for us to reflect? Our reflection will also lead us to this crucial understanding: Just as Allah is absolutely perfect in His creation, He is also absolutely perfect in His legislation- in the things He commands us, and in the things He prohibits for us. Allah says,

أَلَا لَهُ ٱلْخَلْقُ وَٱلْأَمْرُ تَبَارَكَ
ٱللَّهُ رَبُّ ٱلْعَـٰلَمِينَ

"Unquestionably, His is the creation and the command; blessed is Allah, Lord of the worlds." [29]

Allah is perfect in every way and thus, He perfectly legislates what is best for us. Wouldn't we then be fooling ourselves if we were to decide that we are only going to follow some of what He says, and abandon other parts?

---

28. Surah Al-Jathiyah [45:13]
29. Surah Al-A'raf [7:54]

ACTIVITY

HOW WOULD YOU ADVISE?

Ahmed is an ambitious young working man whom you've met at a conference. He casually mentions his thoughts on work-life balance and says, "You know, because of the time and place we live in, I really don't think it fits our lifestyle anymore to pray five times a day. Maybe we should start thinking of making things easier on ourselves and praying only when we can." How would you use the knowledge you have of Allah to give Ahmed the right advice? When we make these meaningful connections between Allah's perfection and how we choose to live, we afford our minds the freedom of following our *fitrah*, and we tether our hearts to the love of whatever Allah loves.

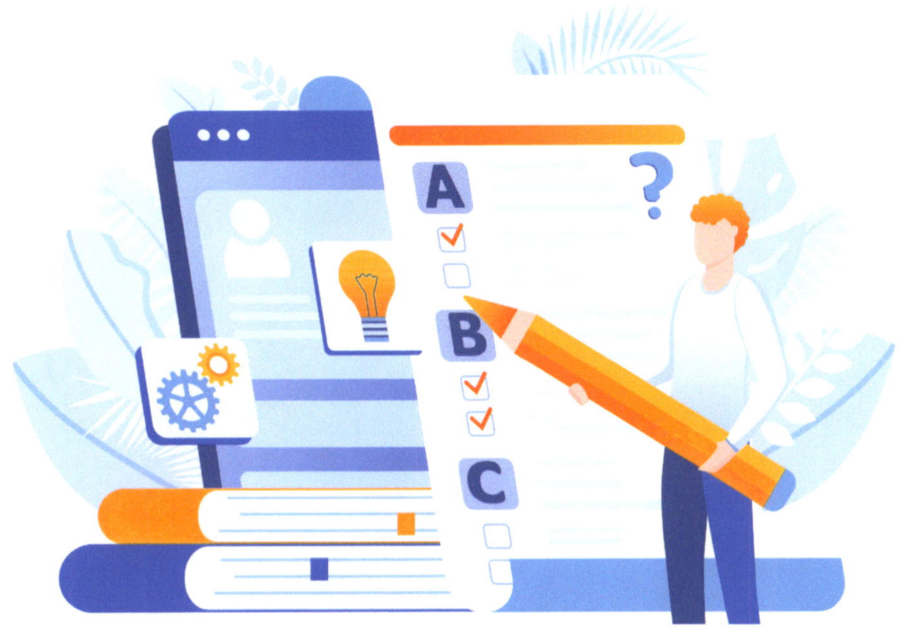

CHAPTER 6

REVIEW AND REFLECT QUESTIONS

1

How can true faith be to believe in what Allah has told us to be true, regardless of whether science has already proven it or not?

2

"Mother Nature" is a term that personifies nature and its nurturing aspects in the form of a mother. These notions of nature being godly all admit that someone or something is in charge of creation. Why is it completely wrong and against our aqeedah to use this term?

3

How does common sense or your natural intuition come into play when deciding on whether something should be believed or not? Give an example of a situation in which we should use our common sense.

CHAPTER 7

INCREDIBLE & PRECISE CREATION

" Then Do They Not Reflect Upon the Qur'an? "[30]

Abdul-Baseer has decided he needs to spend more time with the *Qur'an*, because he's been feeling a little empty lately. He begins reading it with the translation of the meanings and thinks, ***this is so beautifully described.*** Then, that thought carries him up to loftier ones, where he then begins to ponder the incredible power of Allah. Abdul Baseer starts to realize why he's been feeling so empty. He just doesn't take the time to sit alone with his Lord and reflect. He is then moved to ponder further: *This amazing Lord of mine, Who has sent this Qur'an, Who has created this entire universe.... He wants* ***me*** *to draw closer to Him through His words. He wants* ***me*** *to be guided and attain the splendors of Paradise. He wishes for* ***me*** *to be saved from any torment in the Hellfire. He is so powerful and yet, so merciful. He is able to destroy and create in an instant and yet, has given me so many chances to come back to Him when I've fallen short. Oh Allah, forgive me for my shortcomings, and guide me to what pleases You.*

30. Surah Muhammad [47:24]

Sometimes, we forget to simply sit and reflect within ourselves - a beloved act of worship to Allah called ***taddabbur.*** The above stream of thought is something we need not study books for, or have a degree to understand. *Taddabbur* is something that everyone is capable of doing, if he just allows himself the opportunity. One of the easiest ways to strengthen our belief in Allah is to reflect on the magnificence of His creation, especially through those descriptions found in the *Qur'an.* In fact, Allah warns us of being negligent of this beloved deed, as He says in the *Qur'an*:

أَفَلَا يَتَدَبَّرُونَ ٱلْقُرْءَانَ أَمْ عَلَىٰ قُلُوبٍ أَقْفَالُهَا

"Then do they not reflect upon the Qur'an, or are there locks upon [their] hearts?" [31]

Do you remember the short exercise you did at the beginning of the earlier lesson, where you listed the things you knew about an object? How much of what you know about the object is described in the *Qur'an*?

The *Qur'an* often goes into exquisite detail in its descriptions of the creation. This, of course, is because only the Creator of the heavens and earth could describe His creation with such precision, as you will see in the few examples covered in this chapter, *in shaa Allah.* We also have the *sunnah* of the Prophet Muhammad *sallAllahu 'alayhi wa sallam*, which plays an integral part in understanding the deeper meanings of the *Qur'an*. He was the living example of the message of the *Qur'an*, and his sayings open our minds to the insightful meanings therein.

Before we take a closer look, it's important to first be clear about our perspective. While we are encouraged to study creation through the observations of the natural world and its discoveries, we should not make that our standard for ultimate truth. The study of our natural world is an ever-changing field, where theories and discoveries are constantly reexamined and altered with the advent of new theories and discoveries. Thus, we should remember to always look at the evidence from an Islamic perspective; that is, to make the *Qur'an* and *Sunnah* our fixed standard of truth, and to compare what's found against it. For example, we wouldn't say *"I now believe in the Qur'anic description of the stars being in (relative) fixed positions because scientists have discovered it."* Instead, we should say *"I affirm belief in whatever is in the Qur'an, even if science disagrees with it or hasn't yet discovered it."* With that said, let us embark together on a journey through some of these descriptions in the *ayaat* of the *Qur'an,* to deepen our understanding and awe of Allah.

---

31. Surah Muhammad [47:24]

THE IMPORTANCE OF REFLECTION

Ibn 'Umayr *radhiAllahu 'anhu* said to Aisha *radhiAllahu 'anha*: Tell us of the most amazing thing you saw from the Messenger of Allah (blessings and peace of Allah be upon him). Aisha remained silent for a while, then she said: One night he said: *"O Aisha, let me focus on worshipping my Lord this night."* I said: By Allah, I love to be near you, and I love what makes you happy. He got up and did *wudoo'*, then he began to pray. She said: And he kept weeping until his lap became wet. Then he wept and kept weeping until his beard became wet. Then he wept and kept weeping until the ground became wet. Then Bilaal came to call him for prayer, and when he saw him weeping, he said: O Messenger of Allah, why are you weeping when Allah has forgiven you your past and future sins? He said: *"Should I not be a thankful slave."* Last night a verse was revealed to me; woe to the one who recites it and does not reflect (from Surah Ale-Imran *ayaat* 190 and 191): *"Indeed, in the creation of the heavens and the earth and the alternation of the night and the day are signs for those of understanding. Who remember Allah while standing or sitting or [lying] on their sides and give thought to the creation of the heavens and the earth, [saying], 'Our Lord, You did not create this aimlessly; exalted are You [above such a thing]; then protect us from the punishment of the Fire.'"*

The Wonder of Being a Human!

How old is your very first memory? Is it you riding a bike for the first time? Or is it when you named your favorite doll or action figure? What it probably is not, is the time you first learned to crawl, or when you tasted your first bite of mashed food or going back even further, it definitely would not be from the time you spent in the womb before you were born. No doubt, you were a full human being right before birth; but no matter how hard you try, you will never be able to recall any memories from the womb. This is because long-term memory fully develops after about three years of life.

We humans go through incredible physical, emotional, and intellectual transformations from the moment we are conceived to the moment we die. Entering the world as a newborn baby is a feat in its own right; so much so, that Allah describes the transition from womb to birth as a new, different creation. We are utterly helpless as newborns; then, as we learn and grow, we gain strength, knowledge, and independence. But, this does not last

Did you know that your height is the size of 24 of your palms? Try it! The Vitruvian Man is a drawing made by the Italian polymath Leonardo da Vinci in about 1490. It is based on the work of the Roman architect Vitruvius. It shows how perfectly Allah has made and created humans, in perfect proportions. The human body, like many other creations of Allah, is perfectly symmetrical and proportionate. "In every human, a palm is four fingers, a foot is four palms, a cubit is six palms, four cubits make a man, a pace is four cubits, a man is 24 palms and these measurements are in his buildings." Vitruvius 36 BC

Reflecting on Our Creation

forever. This progression carries on and then, soberingly, cycles back- something you've likely witnessed at some point.

Allah says:

أَشُدَّكُمْ وَمِنكُم مَّن يُتَوَفَّىٰ وَمِنكُم مَّن يُرَدُّ إِلَىٰٓ أَرْذَلِ ٱلْعُمُرِ لِكَيْلَا يَعْلَمَ مِنۢ بَعْدِ عِلْمٍ شَيْـًٔا

"And among you is he who is taken in [early] death, and among you is he who is returned to the most decrepit [old] age so that he knows, after [once having knowledge, nothing." [32]

We have to reflect on our own human weakness, in order to remember Allah's *subhaanahu wa ta'aala* power and strength. We are to remember our final return to Him, so that we waste not a moment preparing for it. Allah directs us to reflect on our own selves when He says,

وَفِى أَنفُسِكُمْ أَفَلَا تُبْصِرُونَ وَفِى ٱلْأَرْضِ ءَايَٰتٌ لِّلْمُوقِنِينَ

"And on the earth are signs for the certain [in faith]. And in yourselves. Then will you not see?" [33]

Though a lot can be said and written about the phenomena that color our humanity, let us focus on just the very initial stages and explore how the *Qur'an* beautifully presents it.

---

32. Surah Al-Hajj [22:5]
33. Surah Adh-Dhariyaat [51:20-21]

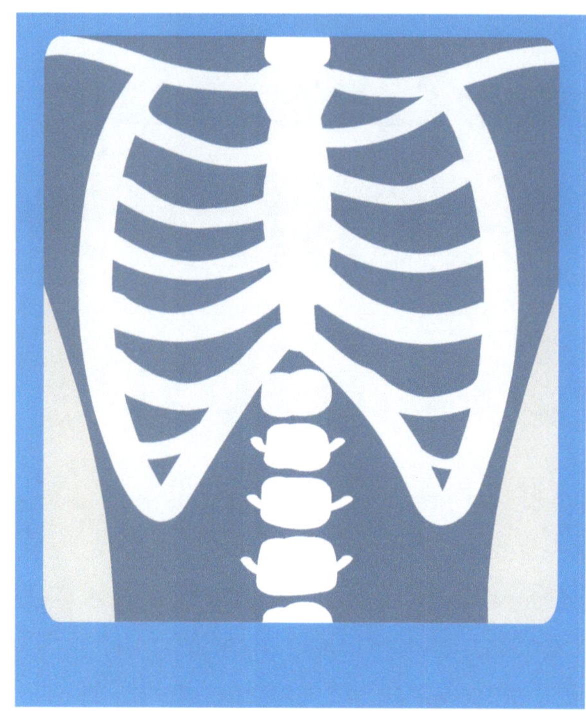

The stages of human creation is a spectacle worthy of pause and reflection.

Descriptions of Human Development in The *Quran*

The description of human development in the *Qur'an* is quite remarkably accurate - even as science and medicine were only properly equipped to explore with ultrasound recently. However, Allah mentions it in precise detail:

مُضْغَةً فَخَلَقْنَا ٱلْمُضْغَةَ عِظَٰمًا فَكَسَوْنَا ٱلْعِظَٰمَ لَحْمًا

"And We made [from] the lump, bones, and We covered the bones with flesh" [34]

The Human Body: A Masterpiece

Have you ever wondered about the shapes and functions in your own body? Say perhaps, how the fingers on your hands are symmetrical and bend just the right way to help you accomplish basic motor skills? Or how each chamber of your heart pumps precisely at the right time, without fail, without you controlling it, even while you sleep soundly in your bed? Sometimes we only appreciate what we have when something goes wrong, or when we get sick. A smart person will train himself to appreciate the blessings he has before losing them. From the most basic to the most complex aspects of being human, we are a living example of Allah's favor upon the creation.

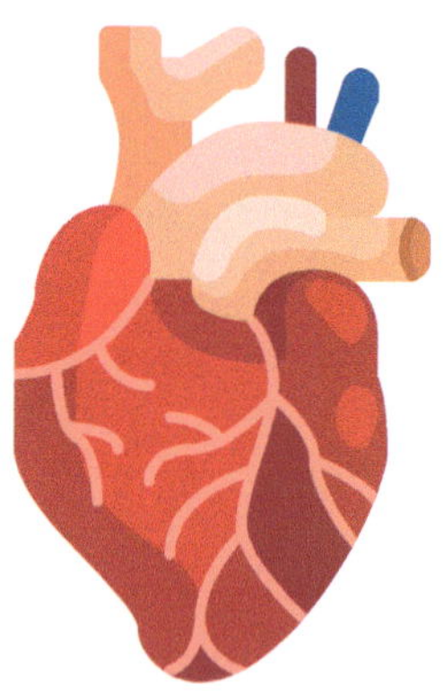

34. Surah Al-Mu?minun [23:14]

The Honey Bee

One of the most intelligent creatures that lives on this earth is no larger than your pinky finger and can deliver a powerful sting if needed. It is the honey bee. Not only do honey bees produce an incredible variety of flavors and colors of honey, but they actually have one of the most sophisticated social structures known to exist in nature. They also play an important role in producing the highest quality fruit and vegetables that we grow and consume. Have you ever observed how a honey bee drifts from flower to flower, drinking its nectar? You may have learned how this is actually the way bees pollinate our flowers and agriculture, and without them, we would not have the vast variety of nuts and produce we enjoy regularly. Allah has made the honey bee one of the most important ways for us to receive our sustenance in this world.

Which other amazing and miraculous animals does Allah mention in the Qu'ran? Give details about its special abilities and significance.

What you may have not known, however, is that **all** of these worker bees - those who forage for nectar in the fields, those who clean the hive, those who feed the other bees, and those who guard and protect the hive - are female. Allah has created each caste of bees in the hierarchy knowing precisely its own role in the colony. Each special feature of the bee is necessary and perfectly tailored for the roles the caste members serve. The leader of the entire colony is the queen bee, who has her own special physical features and role. If not for Allah who has created them, how else would each and every bee know exactly what its role was, with colonies across the world functioning exactly the same way and designed with such uniformity?

Hexagon Makes You Think!

Have you ever seen how a beehive is structured? The hive consists of thousands of tiny closely packed hexagon-shaped cells called a honeycomb. What is fascinating is that this shape is the most suitable for building, as it is still used in modern architecture.

"Why hexagons, though? It's a simple matter of geometry. If you want to pack together cells that are identical in shape and size so that

they fill all of a flat plane, only three regular shapes (with all sides and angles identical) will work: equilateral triangles, squares, and hexagons. Of these, hexagonal cells require the least total length of wall, compared with triangles or squares of the same area. So it makes sense that bees would choose hexagons, since making wax costs them energy, and they will want to use up as little as possible—just as builders might want to save on the cost of bricks." [35]

- Philip Ball

It is as if the honeybee has studied and mastered the knowledge of geometry. She knows to avoid the triangle due to its sharp corners that render that space unusable, and the square due to its longer walls and thus the need to spend more energy to produce greater amounts of wax. Did the honeybee have to study architecture or learn how to build from its bee elders? If it were a learned behavior, we would see a great variance in the hives from colony to colony. Who else but Allah, the Creator of the heavens and the earth, could inspire the honeybee to construct such a uniform, architectural marvel that perfectly serves its purpose?

Description of The Honeybee in The Quran

وَأَوْحَىٰ رَبُّكَ إِلَى ٱلنَّحْلِ أَنِ ٱتَّخِذِى مِنَ
ٱلْجِبَالِ بُيُوتًا وَمِنَ ٱلشَّجَرِ وَمِمَّا يَعْرِشُونَ

"And your Lord inspired to the bee, "Take for yourself among the mountains, houses, and among the trees and [in] that which they construct." [36]

---

35. **"Patterns in Nature: Why the Natural World Looks the Way It Does,"** *by Philip Ball, published by The University of Chicago Press 2016*
36. Surah An-Nahl [16:68]

The description of the honey bee occurs in just two *ayaat* of the *Qur'an,* but from these *ayaat* we can extract many points of benefit. Allah first gives us a glimpse of how He instructs the bee to build the home, using a feminine pronoun in the word ٱتَّخِذِى. This is significant because the use of the feminine pronoun indicates that Allah inspires the female bee to build the hive. Scientists have also affirmed this fact as they also discovered through field observations and testing that the bees who build the hive, and in fact all of the worker bees, are female.

These builder bees construct elaborate hives using wax and as Allah continues in the ayah, they do so in the sides of mountains, in the trees, and in that which they construct (of hives). Then, again the feminine pronoun is used to instruct the worker bees to eat from all the fruits and follow the ways their Lord laid down for them. As we've already discussed, all of the worker bees who forage in the fields and eat the nectar are known to be female.

What it's All About: Honey!

Now, let's examine what the honeybee is perhaps most known for: making honey! Did you know that honey has been used as medicine for more than 4,000 years? [37] Scientists and doctors have written extensively about the antibacterial properties of honey, as well as its ability to fight cancer and heart disease as an antioxidant. They have also described how the various delicious types of honey we extract from the bees differ in color based on what the bee consumed, and that it is produced in the stomach of the bee to yield the sweet, syrup-like liquid. This fact is also

37. The first written reference to honey, a Sumerian tablet writing, dating back to 2100-2000 BCE, mentions honey's use as a drug and an ointment.

mentioned in the *Qur'an.* Allah says,

يَخْرُجُ مِنۢ بُطُونِهَا شَرَابٌ مُّخْتَلِفٌ أَلْوَٰنُهُۥ فِيهِ شِفَآءٌ لِّلنَّاسِ ۗ

*"**There emerges from their bellies** a drink, varying in colors, in which there is healing for people."* [38]

After the worker bees gather nectar from various plants, they store it in their stomach until they reach the hive, where the vomit it into the honeycomb. Though it sounds pretty off-putting, it is actually essential to the curative properties of honey. Bees' stomachs have a special enzyme, which is added to the honey when the nectar is regurgitated. The enzyme and nectar mix to produce hydrogen peroxide which is a common household product used to disinfect cuts, scrapes, and kills harmful bacteria. There have been several scientific studies done on the healing properties of honey. This pure, sweet product made by the honeybee can safely remedy an array of ailments without any fear of side effects: as a wound disinfectant, as an antibiotic, in treating ulcers of the stomach, as an anti-inflammatory agent, and for many other uses. [39] It can also act as a preservative for food, as it slows the growth of bacteria and thus prevents food spoilage. Did you know that honey is the only food that never spoils?

38. Surah An-Nahl [16:69]
39. Honey: Its Medicinal Property and Antibacterial Activity- Mandal MD and Mandal S. Asian Pacific Journal of Tropical Biomedicine.

Reason without Revelation

Reason without the divine Revelation (*Qur'an* and the *Sunnah*) is impractical. In other words, using your mind without authentic belief is like using your eyes without light. [40]

In order to understand the danger of using reason without the guidance of divine Revelation is like standing in the middle of a vast garden, with lofty emerald trees and bright colorful flora, glittering under the dazzling sun. Both beauty and danger surround you, for every brilliant color, vivid pattern, and unique texture of your surroundings is a menace of equal measure: a sharp thorn, an upraised root, or a venomous insect that lurks in the artistry of it all. Now imagine, you set out to navigate this delicate gardenscape, but suddenly, all of the light is taken away. Your vision has always been sharp, but what use is that now? Without any light, even perfect eyesight becomes useless. You now remain in total darkness, unable to perceive the beauty that exists around you, and left without sight of the dangers that may harm you.

40. Adapted from the quote of Ibn Taymiyyah *rahmimahullah*.

This metaphor is like that of the one who has the ability to reason, but cannot do so because he is not given the proper guidance. In this analogy sun is representing the *Qur'an,* [41] which is the source of guidance. This source gives light, or faith, to the one trying to understand this reality. If you walk in this garden without the light of the sun to avail you, you benefit not from the breathtaking beauty that surrounds you, and are bound to be stricken by the dangers hidden beneath that beauty. The one who chooses not to be guided by the light of the *Qur'an* will not truly benefit from his existence here on earth, and he puts himself in grave danger of a terrible afterlife. Allah mentions about them;

أَوْ كَظُلُمَـٰتٍ فِى بَحْرٍ لُّجِّىٍّ يَغْشَىٰهُ مَوْجٌ مِّن فَوْقِهِۦ مَوْجٌ مِّن فَوْقِهِۦ سَحَابٌ ظُلُمَـٰتٌۢ بَعْضُهَا فَوْقَ بَعْضٍ إِذَآ أَخْرَجَ يَدَهُۥ لَمْ يَكَدْ يَرَىٰهَا وَمَن لَّمْ يَجْعَلِ ٱللَّهُ لَهُۥ نُورًا فَمَا لَهُۥ مِن نُّورٍ

"Or [they are] like darknesses within an unfathomable sea which is covered by waves, upon which are waves, over which are clouds - darknesses, some of them upon others. When one puts out his hand therein], he can hardly see it. And he whom Allah has not granted light - for him there is no light." [42]

41. And, by extension, the *Sunnah.*
42. Surah An-Nur [24:40]

Does Allah Compel Us to Go Astray?

Does Allah compels a person to go astray, since He chooses not to grant him light [guidance]? Certainly not! It means that over and over again, Allah has shown him clear signs of His marvelous creation and of His magnificent revelation and yet, the person chose not to see them. He put his faith in something other than Allah, and thus sealed his own heart from letting the light of guidance enter it. Just as Allah says,

وَنُقَلِّبُ أَفْـِٔدَتَهُمْ وَأَبْصَـٰرَهُمْ كَمَا لَمْ يُؤْمِنُوا۟ بِهِۦٓ أَوَّلَ مَرَّةٍ وَنَذَرُهُمْ فِى طُغْيَـٰنِهِمْ يَعْمَهُونَ

"And We will turn away their hearts and their eyes just as they refused to believe in it the first time. And We will leave them in their transgression, wandering blindly." [43]

Recall the story of Prophet Nuh *'alayhis salaam* and his disbelieving son. His son chose not to heed his father's warning about the impending flood sent by Allah to punish those who disbelieved and instead exclaimed, *"I will take refuge on a mountain to protect me from the water."* [44] He gave blind authority to his limited, imperfect intellect, while Prophet Nuh *'alayhis salaam* held fast to believe in his perfect Lord and embarked upon the ark. We know the ending to this story. Who was saved from the flood, and who perished in its deadly waters?

There is much comfort in the fact that as long as the sun rises in the east, the proof of Allah will remain. There is proof in His creation and proof in His revelation. He has promised to preserve the final message so that we have a clear, practical roadmap to a meaningful life. While Allah will surely test us with the intellect He has given us, He also guarantees the best return for using it properly. If we use it with our fitrah and we are sincere in seeking guidance, He will surely keep us on the straight path.

43. Surah Al-An'aam [6:110]
44. Surah Hud [11:43]

ACTIVITY

Mr. McIntyre is a man who has reached a very old age. Gradually, he begins to lose memory of things like his children's names, or the address where he's lived for decades. His physical strength weakens, but he is too ashamed to ask for help in mundane tasks like putting on his own shoes. His mental aptitude declines, whereby just thinking about what he will do that day exhausts him. His general vigor is reduced to almost nothing, such that he prefers to stay sitting in the same reliable, tattered old chair, unless there is a real need to move because it just makes him so tired. Poor Mr. McIntyre is now completely dependent on others, just as he was when he was a newborn baby.

Imagine that this old, frail man encroaching upon the end of his days, has for his entire adult life, denied that he has a Creator to answer to. He once felt himself invincible, and never could have imagined himself to be this weak and vulnerable. Now, and in this condition, the last chapter of Mr. McIntyre's life is about to conclude and his book is soon to be forever closed. Take a few seconds and think about the emotional response you had reading this scenario. What was your initial reaction? Did that feeling change once you reached the end, or did it stay the same?

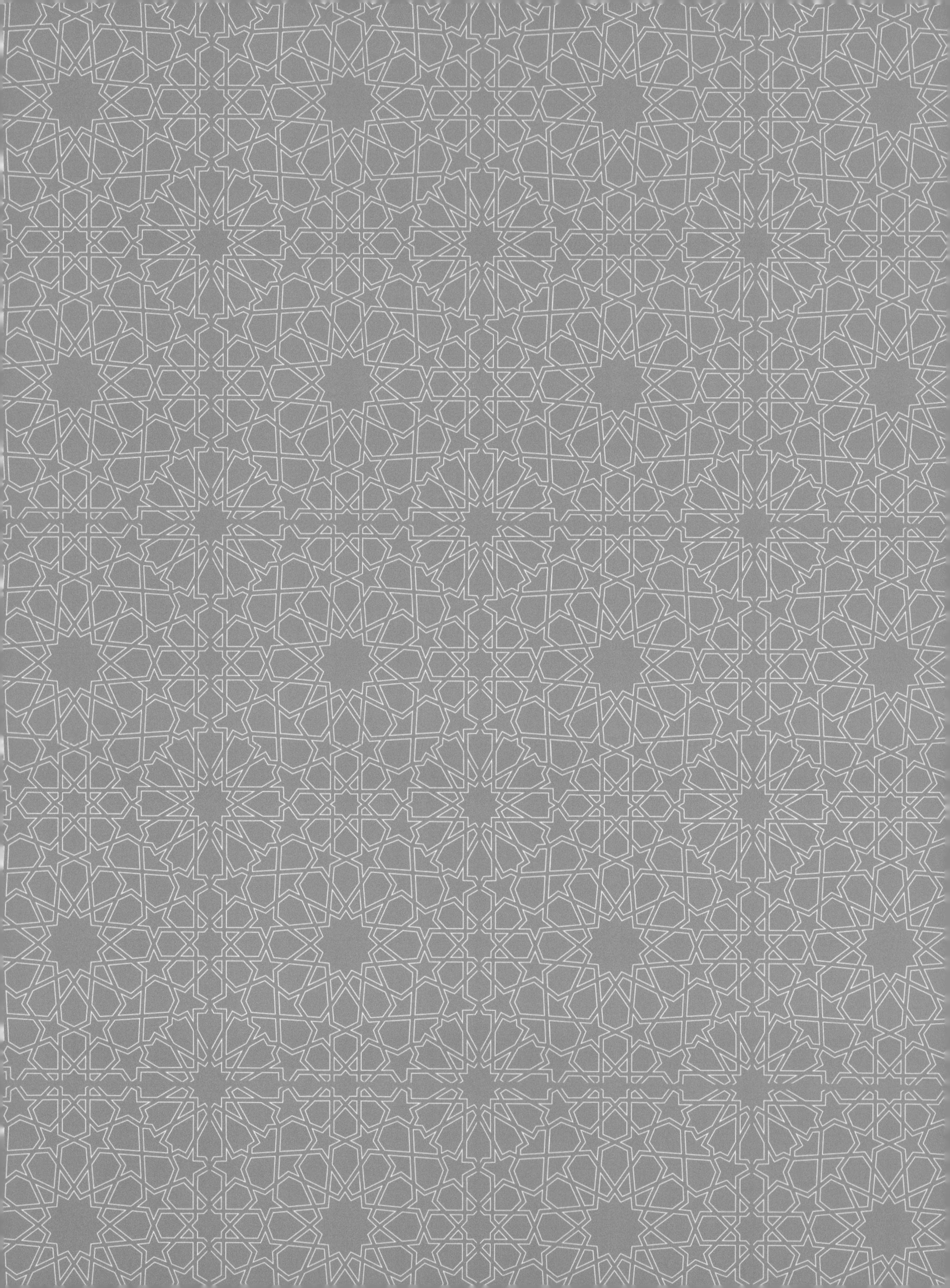

UNIT 3

ALLAH IN MY LIFE

UNIT 3

Important Vocabulary

Isti'anah
To seek help from Allah.

Istisharah
To consult with others.

Rabb
Allah; The sole Creator, Owner, Master, Sustainer, and Nurturer of all creation.

Salatul Istikhara
To ask Allah to guide you by praying a special prayer for guidance.

Tarbiyah
To nurture, bring up or raise.

Tawakkul
To depend on Allah alone.

Tawheed
Maintaining the Oneness of Allah in His Lordship, His Names and Attributes, as well as in worship in our daily lives.

Tawheed Al-Asmaai-was-Sifaat
Allah's Oneness in His Names and Attributes.

Tawheed Ar Ruboobiyyah
Allah's Oneness in His Lordship.

Tawheed Al-Uloohiyyah
Allah's Oneness in His worship.

TABLE OF CONTENTS

UNIT 3 | ALLAH IN MY LIFE

Essential Questions

This unit is designed to help answer the following questions.

1. Will submitting to Allah and knowing our purpose in life guarantee us a sense of peace?
2. How does belief in the Oneness of Allah in His Lordship impact our mental and emotional well-being?
3. How does knowing that Allah is One in His Lordship affect our daily choices in life?
4. What do I gain by striving for Allah's love? What do I lose?
5. How do superstitious beliefs, charms, and amulets affect our beliefs?

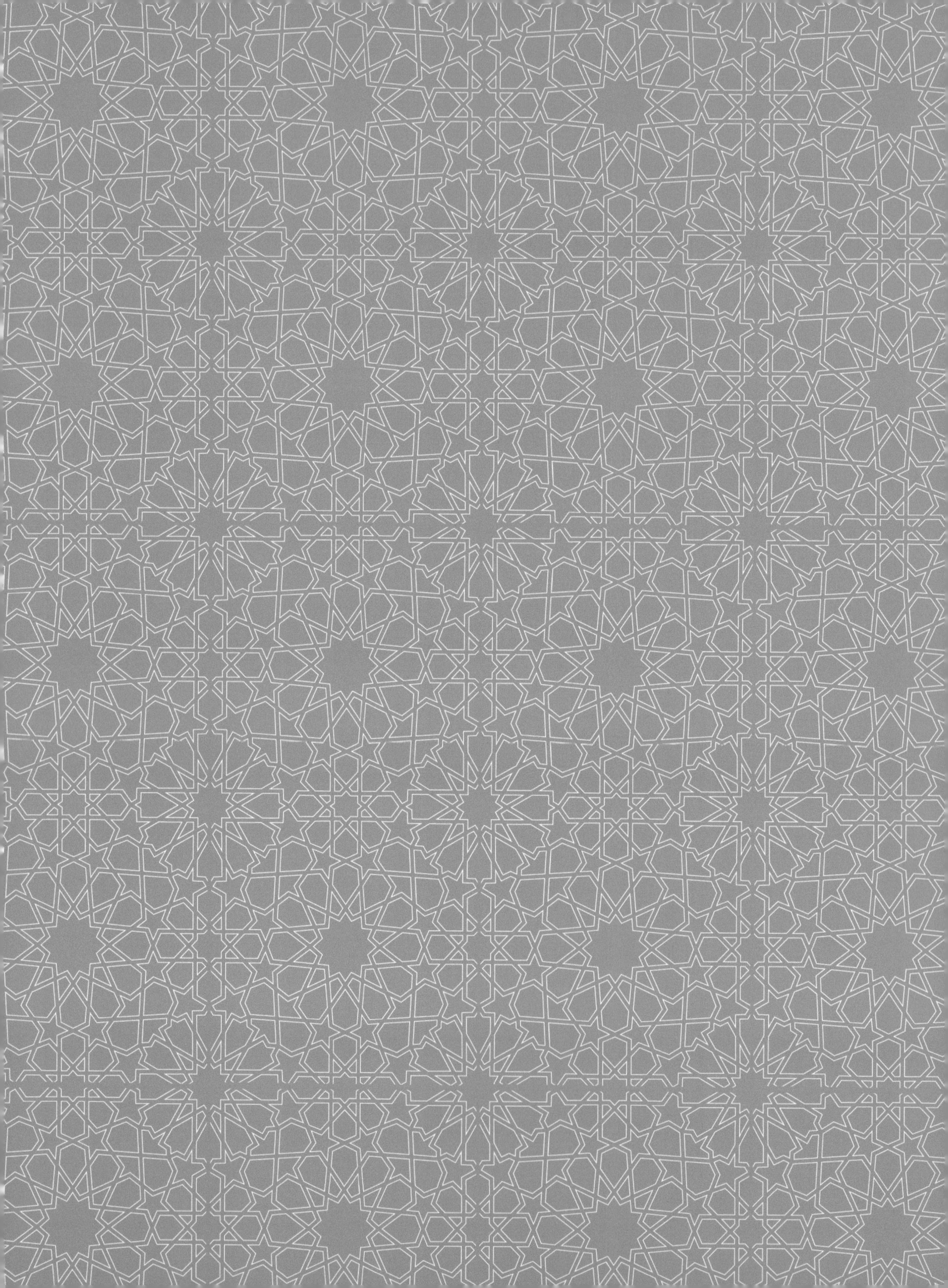

CHAPTER 8

ALLAH, ONE AND ONLY

Introduction to *Tawheed*

If you want to love Allah, you have to know Allah. The only way to truly know Allah is to understand *Tawheed*. *Tawheed* is defined as maintaining the oneness of Allah in His Lordship, His Names and Attributes, as well as in His worship in our daily lives.

EMBRACING OUR PURPOSE

We know that Allah created this amazing earth, our entire universe, and all of humanity for a profound purpose: **To worship Allah alone** or, in other words, to establish *tawheed* [Allah's oneness] in our lives. While many people spend a lifetime searching for their purpose and yearning for peace, Allah tells us our purpose in the *Qur'an,*

وَمَا خَلَقْتُ ٱلْجِنَّ وَٱلْإِنسَ إِلَّا لِيَعْبُدُونِ

"I did not create the jinn and mankind except to worship Me." [1]

1. Surah Adh-Dhariyaat [51:56]

Finding Peace

How can we find peace knowing our purpose in life? Allah has also informed us that living according to this correct belief in Him is the way to achieving inner peace and contentment in this life as well as eternal happiness in the next:

ٱلَّذِينَ ءَامَنُوا۟ وَلَمْ يَلْبِسُوٓا۟ إِيمَـٰنَهُم بِظُلْمٍ أُو۟لَـٰٓئِكَ لَهُمُ ٱلْأَمْنُ وَهُم مُّهْتَدُونَ

"Those who believe and do not mix their belief with wrongdoing will have security and will be rightly-guided." [2]

The Prophet Muhammad *sallAllahu 'alayhi wa sallam* explained that wrongdoing in this ayaah refers to *shirk* which is associating a partner with Allah in worship.

How Can Tawheed Benefit Us?

ACHIEVING SUCCESS

Allah defines success in the *Qur'an*,

مَنْ عَمِلَ صَـٰلِحًا مِّن ذَكَرٍ أَوْ أُنثَىٰ وَهُوَ مُؤْمِنٌ فَلَنُحْيِيَنَّهُۥ حَيَوٰةً طَيِّبَةً وَلَنَجْزِيَنَّهُمْ أَجْرَهُم بِأَحْسَنِ مَا كَانُوا۟ يَعْمَلُونَ

"Whoever does righteousness, whether male or female, while he is a believer, We will surely allow him to live a good life, and We will certainly give them their reward [in the Hereafter] according to the best of what they used to do." [3]

---

2. Surah Al-An'aam [6:82]
3. Surah An-Nahl [16:97]

Success with Allah is not how some of us view success. If you were prompted to write about a successful person, you may think of Jeff Bezos, Elon Musk or Mark Zuckerberg. We would not necessarily think of someone who was homeless or accidentally killed a man and fled the country. Yet, that is part of the heroic story of Prophet Musa *'alayhi as-salaam* as he achieved success with Allah.

Do the stories of the prophets *'alayhum us-salaam* rush to our minds when we think of success? If not, perhaps the problem is with our thinking. Why do we think of success in the worldly sense? A truly accomplished life is what Allah defines as successful and it will manifest in the *akhirah* (hereafter).

Forgiveness

Who among us does not need forgiveness? Even our beloved Prophet *sallAllahu 'alayhi wa sallam* who was promised *Jannah* sought forgiveness sincerely. *Shirk* is a major sin and if a person does not ask for forgiveness and change their ways, they are on a precarious path.

Our Prophet *sallAllahu 'alayhi wa sallam* informed us that Allah said,

وَمَنْ أَتَانِي يَمْشِي أَتَيْتُهُ هَرْوَلَةً وَمَنْ لَقِيَنِي بِقُرَابِ الْأَرْضِ خَطِيئَةً لَا يُشْرِكُ بِي شَيْئًا لَقِيتُهُ بِمِثْلِهَا مَغْفِرَةً

"Whoever meets me (on the Day of Judgment) with sins which are enough to fill the earth, but has never associated any partners with Me, I will meet him/her with an equivalent amount of forgiveness." [4]

Protection From Hellfire

The Prophet *sallAllahu 'alayhi wa sallam* explained that our protection and eternal bliss in the next life depends on our sincere *tawheed*.

فَإِنَّ اللَّهَ حَرَّمَ عَلَى النَّارِ مَنْ قَالَ لَا إِلَهَ إِلَّا اللَّهُ يَبْتَغِي بِذَلِكَ وَجْهَ اللَّهِ

"Allah has surely prohibited the fire (from touching) the one who says ' There is none worthy of worship but Allah', seeking Allah's Face alone." [5]

Keeping firm to our beliefs in t*awheed* is the best protection from the Hell-Fire.

---

4. Sahih Muslim
5. Sahih Al-Bukhari

Holding The Anchor of Our Faith: *Tawheed*

Now that we have learned a little more about the importance of *tawheed*, let's evaluate ourselves. Do we worship Allah alone completely and wholeheartedly today? Nowadays, people favor celebrities, politicians, social media influencers, leaders, and friends as supreme idols. Many prefer to follow a different way of life than the one Allah has gifted us with. Their likes and dislikes are given importance over Allah's likes and dislikes.

Some people may honestly think: Well, I don't worship idols, and I pray and fast, but I can't say I feel peace and contentment. Why then, don't I feel a profound purpose in my life? Am I missing something? To fully understand *tawheed* and its full implications on our day-to-day lives, let's continue to evaluate ourselves as we answer some critical questions:

- **What** does *"establishing tawheed in our lives"* look like?
- **What** does *"worshipping Allah"* truly mean?
- **How** exactly does this give us purpose and peace in our day-to-day life?

The answers to these questions will become clear when we consider what *tawheed* is composed of. *Tawheed* is inclusive of three areas, as specified by Allah in the following *ayaah*,

ذَٰلِكُمُ ٱللَّهُ رَبُّكُمْ لَآ إِلَـٰهَ إِلَّا هُوَ خَـٰلِقُ كُلِّ
شَىْءٍ فَٱعْبُدُوهُ وَهُوَ عَلَىٰ كُلِّ شَىْءٍ وَكِيلٌ

"That is Allah, your Lord! There is no god worthy of worship except Him. He is the Creator of all things, so worship Him alone. And He is the Maintainer of everything." [6]

1. **Allah's Oneness in His Lordship - *Tawheed Ur-Ruboobiyyah***
2. **Allah's Oneness in His Names and Attributes - *Tawheed Ul-Asmaai-was-Sifaat***
3. **Allah's Oneness in His worship - *Tawheed Ul-Uloohiyyah.***

We will continue to discuss these three aspects of *tawheed* in the next few chapters and units.

---

6. Surah Al-An'aam [6:102]

CHAPTER 8

REVIEW AND REFLECT QUESTIONS

1

What does *Tawheed* mean to you in the practical sense? When we say "*Allah is our only Rabb*", what comes to mind?

2

Think of something you really want to achieve. How will you apply *Tawheed Ar- Ruboobiyyah*, making Allah the only Rabb in your heart before, during, and after your actions? Be specific.

3

Think of a hardship you or someone you know went through. Despite the hardship, were there any blessings that came up after the valuable lesson?

4

Meet Ali Banat: Ali was a young Australian Muslim businessman of Lebanese descent. Through his self- built security and electrical company, Ali quickly became a successful millionaire before the age of thirty and built a reputation for a luxurious, materialistic lifestyle. He spent his twenties traveling the world and accumulating diamond- encrusted watches, multiple Ferraris, and a limited-edition wardrobe from high- end brands like Gucci and Louis Vuitton. He persisted in his materialistic pursuits until, one day, Ali was diagnosed with stage-four cancer. He called his diagnosis, *"the gift"* that opened his eyes to the Reality of Allah and His existence inspired his spiritual awakening. Ali died in Ramadan at the age of thirty-six. Explain in your own words how his cancer was a gift to him from Allah?

CHAPTER 9

ALLAH NURTURES US

Tawheed Ur-Ruboobiyyah: Allah's Oneness in His Lordship

Tawheed Ur-Ruboobiyyah is an aspect of *tawheed* that means to firmly believe that Allah is the only *Rabb* and to act on that belief. Although *Rabb* is translated as *"Lord,"* it actually means much more in Arabic. It means that Allah is the sole Creator, Owner, Master, Sustainer, and Nurturer of all creation. So not only did Allah alone create everything in existence, but He is the only One who decides, controls, and decrees what happens in the universe. Nothing can happen in the universe, good or bad, except what He allows and causes to happen. Allah mentions in the *Qur'an*,

ٱللَّهُ خَـٰلِقُ كُلِّ شَىْءٍ ۖ وَهُوَ عَلَىٰ كُلِّ شَىْءٍ وَكِيلٌ

"Allah created all things and He is Wakeel (the Maintainer) over everything." [7]

He is the only One who can give or withhold His blessings. He can guide and allow someone to be misguided. He can decree a problem and also grant its solution. Furthermore, everything He does in this universe is based on His infinite wisdom, knowledge, and mercy. It is based on a perfect plan.

7. Surah Az-Zumar [39:62]

Believing that Allah is the *only* Rabb, then, means believing that anything and everything that occurs, be it good or bad, **is by His will and decree**. It means that no benefit or harm can come to us except by His permission. Success, relief, happiness, wealth, sickness, and health are from Him.

How Does Allah Nurture Us?

We explained how Allah is the Creator, Owner, Master, and Sustainer of the world. Now we will explain what "nurturer" means in more detail. The word "***Rabb***" is similar to the word "***tarbiyah***", which is the same Arabic word used to refer to a parent raising or upbringing his/her child. ***Tarbiyah*** means to nurture, bring up or raise. In this context, a good parent is concerned with his or her child's well-being and takes care of the child's physical needs. However, a caring parent will go beyond and also nurture his or her child emotionally and spiritually as well. They would keep their child in a positive environment, may go out of their way to surround the child with beneficial friends, and avoid harmful ones. They would also encourage their children to hear inspiring lectures and stories which will fill their hearts with Allah's love. This is an example of a well-rounded, truly concerned parent.

Similarly, Allah cares for us even more than a concerned parent. Everything Allah does for us is out of care and concern for our best interest and our personal growth. He allows us to go through certain experiences in order to grow, learn about Him, and gradually increase our *iman*. Even if something bad happens, it is for a reason that is ultimately in our best interest.

Types of Tarbiyah

Allah has two types of tarbiyah:
a general tarbiyah and a special tarbiyah.
We will expand more on these topics below.

1 GENERAL *TARBIYAH*

General *Tarbiyah* is the *tarbiyah* by which He nurtures and takes care of all of His creation, whether they are believers or disbelievers, righteous or sinful, grateful or ungrateful. This simply means He alone created everyone, grants them life and death, decides on their affairs, provides for them, and grants them various blessings. These blessings can include health, money, a home, provisions, abilities, education, success in this world, and much more.

That's why Allah introduces Himself as the *"The Rabb of all the Worlds"* in Surah Al-Fatihah,

"All Praise and Thanks are due to Allah, the Lord of the Worlds." [8]

2 SPECIAL *TARBIYAH*

Special *Tarbiyah* is the *tarbiyah* which is especially for His beloved, believing servants. He takes special care of them emotionally and spiritually as a reward for their belief in Him and acceptance of His guidance. If we believe in Him and try to seek His pleasure, He inspires us to do what will increase our *iman*. He nurtures our hearts with knowledge and love of Him, makes good deeds easy for us, guides us to all that is good for us in our *deen* and *dunya* (worldly life), and protects us from what is harmful. He also *"raises us"* by putting us through situations which will strengthen us, bring us closer to Him, nurture our good qualities, and rid us of our bad ones. In other words, if we strive to seek His pleasure, He will take us under His special *tarbiyah* and develop us in the best way, the way which will bring us closest to Him and allow us to reach our highest potential.

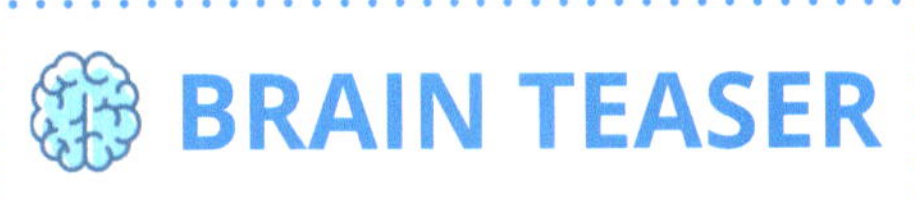

What other *"worlds"* can you think of that Allah is the *Rabb* of?

8. Surah Al-Fatiha [1:2]

Allah also introduced himself to both the Prophet Musa *'alayhis salaam* and to the Prophet Muhammad *sallAllahu 'alayhi wa sallam* with the word *Rabb*.

إِنِّىٓ أَنَا۠ رَبُّكَ فَٱخْلَعْ نَعْلَيْكَ
إِنَّكَ بِٱلْوَادِ ٱلْمُقَدَّسِ طُوًى

"It is truly I, I am your Lord. Remove your sandals, for you are in the sacred valley of Tuwa." [9]

ٱقْرَأْ بِٱسْمِ رَبِّكَ ٱلَّذِى خَلَقَ

"Read! In the name of your Lord Who created you." [10]

It is also why many of the *du'aas* highlighted in the *Qur'an* begin specifically with *"Rabbi"* which is *"My Rabb"* instead of, for example, *"Ya Allah"* or *"Allahumma"* which mean *"O Allah."* It is as if they are calling out quickly and in desperation, saying, *"Since you are My Rabb, who alone is in control and takes special care of me, protect me from this harm."*

Let's venture on to see why the prophets implored Allah using His name Ar-Rabb and the effects His special *Ruboobiyyah* had on their lives. In each example, how does Allah's *Ruboobiyyah* manifest itself?

How many du'aas can you find in the Qur'an that begin with "Rabbi" or "Ya Rabb"?

9. Surah Taha [20:12]
10. Surah Al-'Alaq [96:1]

Allah's Special Tarbiyah in the Lives of the Prophets *`alayhumus salaam*

The prophets *'alayhumus salaam* were the greatest practical examples of what a firm belief in Allah's *Ruboobiyyah* looks like. Let's take a look at how one of the prophets dealt with what seemed to be impossible. Prophet Zakariyyah *'alayhis salaam* and his wife had reached a very old age, making it impossible for them to have children. He longed for a child and wanted to leave the legacy of *tawheed* behind after his death. One day, he saw Maryam *'alayhas salaam* in her isolated place of worship with fruits which were out of season. Surprised, he asked her about it.

قَالَتْ هُوَ مِنْ عِندِ ٱللَّهِ إِنَّ ٱللَّهَ يَرْزُقُ مَن يَشَآءُ بِغَيْرِ حِسَابٍ

"...She said, it is from Allah. Truly, Allah provides to whomever He wills without limit." [11]

Her response served as a strong prompt to Prophet Zakariyyah *'alayhis salaam* that Allah can create whatever He wishes and provide the unimaginable.

هُنَالِكَ دَعَا زَكَرِيَّا رَبَّهُۥ قَالَ رَبِّ هَبْ لِى مِن لَّدُنكَ ذُرِّيَّةً طَيِّبَةً إِنَّكَ سَمِيعُ ٱلدُّعَآءِ

"At that moment, Zakariyyah called on his Rabb, saying, 'My Rabb, grant me especially from You righteous offspring. Truly, You are the (only) One who answers prayers!" [12]

Right then and there he made *du'aa*. A lesson that we can learn is that we can be reminded of Allah's special *tarbiyah* by someone who is younger than us, too.

So Allah sent angels to give him the good news of a child, who not only would be righteous but would also be a prophet! Notice how Zakariyyah used Allah's name, "*Ar-Rabb*" in his prayer and how Allah said, "*He called on his Rabb*" not "*on Allah.*" So we see here how a firm belief in Allah's *Ruboobiyyah* leads us to hopefulness and enables us to fulfill our deepest wishes, sooner or later.

---

11. Surah Ale-Imran [03:37]
12. Surah Ale-Imran [03:38]

Only Our Rabb Can Grant Our Deepest Wishes

This example of Prophet Zakariyyah *'alayhis salaam* is preserved timelessly in the *Qur'an* for a reason. The next time you are in a situation that feels completely hopeless, turn to Allah and firmly believe he can make any impossible situation possible. Just remember to ask Him.

Only Our Rabb Can Provide For Us Even When We Have Nothing

When Musa *'alayhis salaam* escaped Egypt after accidentally killing a man, he went to a town called *Madyan*. He found two women in need of help filling water from a well, and he came to their aid. He then retreated to a shaded area and sat alone. He had no money, no family, no support, no income. So he turned to Allah, knowing that because He is the *Rabb*, only He can provide for him. Allah recorded Prophet Musa's *'alayhis salaam du'aa* in the *Qur'an*,

رَبِّ إِنِّى لِمَآ أَنزَلْتَ إِلَىَّ مِنْ خَيْرٍ فَقِيرٌ

"My Rabb, I am truly in desperate need of any good you may send me." [13]

Soon after that, one of the girls approached him for an invitation to meet her father. Musa *'alayhis salaam* explained his situation and the father was very understanding. The father offered his daughter (with her approval) for marriage as well as a stable job with the family. He asked Allah for any provision, and in a single moment, Allah, the Generous *Rabb*, took special care of him! He was provided with a righteous wife, a home, a job, and the support of a loving family. Allah gave him many forms of provisions.

---

13. Surah Al-Qasas [28:24]

Only Our Rabb Can Protect Us From What We Fear

Think of a time you were afraid of someone or something and you found no one to protect you from this fear. Or were you stuck in a situation that seemed to have no way out? How did you feel and what did you do about it? Perhaps the next time this happens to you, you can remember the following stories, which will strengthen your belief that only Allah, our *Rabb*, can and will protect you if you turn to Him.

Musa *'Alayhis salaam* Had a Strong Trust in Allah

When Allah commanded Musa *'alayhis salaam* to take His message of guidance to the Pharaoh in Egypt after having fled, Musa *'alayhis salaam* was naturally scared that he would be killed. He expressed his fears immediately to Allah alone.

قَالَ رَبِّ إِنِّى قَتَلْتُ مِنْهُمْ نَفْسًا فَأَخَافُ أَن يَقْتُلُونِ
وَأَخِى هَٰرُونُ هُوَ أَفْصَحُ مِنِّى لِسَانًا فَأَرْسِلْهُ مَعِىَ
رِدْءًا يُصَدِّقُنِىٓ إِنِّىٓ أَخَافُ أَن يُكَذِّبُونِ

"He said, 'My Rabb, I (accidentally) killed one of them, so I am afraid that they will kill me. And my brother Haroon is more eloquent than I am, so send him with me as a support to confirm (my message) for I also fear that they will call me a liar!' " [14]

Due to Musa *'alayhis salaam's* firm belief that Allah is the only One who can protect Him and because He turned to Him alone, Allah's immediate response was,

14. Surah Al-Qasas [28:33-34]

قَالَ سَنَشُدُّ عَضُدَكَ بِأَخِيكَ وَنَجْعَلُ لَكُمَا سُلْطَٰنًا فَلَا يَصِلُونَ إِلَيْكُمَا بِـَٔايَٰتِنَآ أَنتُمَا وَمَنِ ٱتَّبَعَكُمَا ٱلْغَٰلِبُونَ

"We will certainly strengthen you through your brother and grant you both supremacy so they will not reach you. [It will be] through Our signs; you and those who follow you will be the predominant." [15]

Similarly, when Allah instructed Musa *'alayhis salaam* to take the Children of Israel and escape from the Pharaoh, the Pharaoh followed them with an entourage of his chiefs, commanders, and supporters. Musa *'alayhis salaam* reached a *"dead end"* with the Red Sea in front of him while the Pharaoh and his army were behind him. Terrified, even the followers of Musa *'alayhis salaam* cried out, *"We are going to be overtaken!"* Musa *'alayhis salaam* remained firm,

فَلَمَّا تَرَٰٓءَا ٱلْجَمْعَانِ قَالَ أَصْحَٰبُ مُوسَىٰٓ إِنَّا لَمُدْرَكُونَ

"He said, 'No! Certainly, my Rabb is with me; He will guide me (through this).' " [16]

He was sure that Allah would save him. And indeed, Allah did not disappoint them but fulfilled their hopes out of His special *tarbiyah.* He commanded Musa *'alayhis salaam* to strike the sea with his staff and the sea split open for the Children of Israel to cross, while it drowned the Pharaoh and his soldiers.

---

15. Surah Al-Qasas [28:35]
16. Surah Ash-Shu'araa [26:61-62]

Only Our *Rabb* Can Cure Us

At some point, we have all fallen sick. In severe cases, sometimes even doctors give up on a recovery. However, it's important to remember that only the *Rabb* controls what will happen. He can do anything, even a miraculous recovery, if it is the best for us. He can provide a cure or withhold it. So we need to turn to Him alone with certainty and confidence.

Allah tested Prophet Ayyub *'alayhis salaam* with a particular illness which made everyone besides his wife stay away from him for eighteen years. Yet, he did not give up, and He turned to Allah and prayed sincerely.

وَأَيُّوبَ إِذْ نَادَىٰ رَبَّهُۥٓ أَنِّى مَسَّنِىَ ٱلضُّرُّ
وَأَنتَ أَرْحَمُ ٱلرَّٰحِمِينَ

"And (mention) Ayyub, when he called on his Rabb, 'Truly adversity has afflicted me, and You are the Most Merciful of the merciful."[17]

So Allah responded to his call and cured him completely from his illness.

Only Our *Rabb* Can Cause Others to Love and Respect Us

It is natural to want others to like and accept us. Many people even crave attention and admiration from others. However, believing in Allah's *Ruboobiyyah* means believing He is in control of everything including the hearts of people.

When Allah instructed Prophet Ibrahim *'alayhis salaam* to leave his wife Hajar and his baby Ismail alone in Makkah, he did as instructed. Then he immediately took all his worries and concerns to his ***Rabb***. He knew Allah was the only One who could solve them. He didn't want them to be lonely or to face animosity, rather he wished that people would care for them and support them. He didn't advise his wife on how she should act in order to get people's love and support; instead he prayed to the One who controls people's hearts, and said,

---

17. Surah Al-Anbiyaa [21:83]

رَّبَّنَآ إِنِّىٓ أَسْكَنتُ مِن ذُرِّيَّتِى بِوَادٍ غَيْرِ
ذِى زَرْعٍ عِندَ بَيْتِكَ ٱلْمُحَرَّمِ رَبَّنَا لِيُقِيمُوا۟
ٱلصَّلَوٰةَ فَٱجْعَلْ أَفْـِٔدَةً مِّنَ ٱلنَّاسِ تَهْوِىٓ
إِلَيْهِمْ وَٱرْزُقْهُم مِّنَ ٱلثَّمَرَٰتِ لَعَلَّهُمْ
يَشْكُرُونَ

"My Rabb! I have settled some of my offspring in a barren valley near Your sacred House, our Rabb, so that they may establish prayer. So make some people's hearts gravitate towards them and provide them with some fruits so that they may be grateful." [18]

And as we know today, his *du'aas* were answered. People came by, settled with them, and helped them build a community in *Makkah*.

Allah also informed us in the *Qur'an* that we should not worry about people's love and acceptance but about His. So if your main concern is to please Him rather than His creation, He will cause people to love and respect you. Allah said,

إِنَّ ٱلَّذِينَ ءَامَنُوا۟ وَعَمِلُوا۟ ٱلصَّٰلِحَٰتِ
سَيَجْعَلُ لَهُمُ ٱلرَّحْمَٰنُ وُدًّا

"Indeed those who believe and do righteous deeds, the Most Merciful will grant them love and affection (from Himself and other people)." [19]

18. Surah Ibrahim [14:37]
19. Surah Maryam [19:96]

The Prophet *sallAllahu 'alayhi wa sallam* has told us,

إِنَّ اللَّهَ إِذَا أَحَبَّ عَبْدًا دَعَا جِبْرِيلَ فَقَالَ إِنِّي أُحِبُّ فُلَانًا فَأَحِبَّهُ قَالَ فَيُحِبُّهُ جِبْرِيلُ ثُمَّ يُنَادِي فِي السَّمَاءِ فَيَقُولُ إِنَّ اللَّهَ يُحِبُّ فُلَانًا فَأَحِبُّوهُ فَيُحِبُّهُ أَهْلُ السَّمَاءِ قَالَ ثُمَّ يُوضَعُ لَهُ الْقَبُولُ فِي الْأَرْضِ

"When Allah loves (His) servant, He calls out to Jibreel, 'Truly Allah loves So-and-So, so you should love him.' So Jibreel will love him and call out to the inhabitants of the skies (the angels), 'Certainly, Allah loves So-and-So, so you should love him.' So the inhabitants of the heavens will love him. Then he/she will also be loved and accepted on earth." [20]

مَنْ الْتَمَسَ رِضَا اللَّهِ بِسَخَطِ النَّاسِ كَفَاهُ اللَّهُ مُؤْنَةَ النَّاسِ وَمَنْ الْتَمَسَ رِضَا النَّاسِ بِسَخَطِ اللَّهِ وَكَلَهُ اللَّهُ إِلَى النَّاسِ

The Prophet *sallAllahu 'alayhi wa sallam* also said, *"Whoever sought the pleasure of Allah though it was displeasing to the people then Allah becomes pleased with him, and will make the people please with him, and whoever sought the pleasure of the people though it was displeasing to Allah then Allah becomes displeased with him and will make the people displeased with him."* [21]

As we can see, a firm belief in Allah's *ruboobiyyah* can lead us to peace and contentment in countless ways. If you have a goal, you will know that only Allah can enable you to achieve it, so you turn to Him alone for help and guidance. If someone threatens you, you know that only Allah can protect you, no matter how strong the person may seem. So you turn to Him for protection and He will protect you. If you have a problem which seems insurmountable, you will know that only Allah can provide you the way out, so you turn to Him to save you and He will. Furthermore, you will know that this problem is for your greater good and it may be a blessing in disguise because your *Rabb* only decrees what is for your benefit. In addition, you will not worry about whether or not people accept you because you realize that Allah controls His entire creation, even the hearts of people.

20. Sahih Al-Bukhari
21. At-Tirmidhi

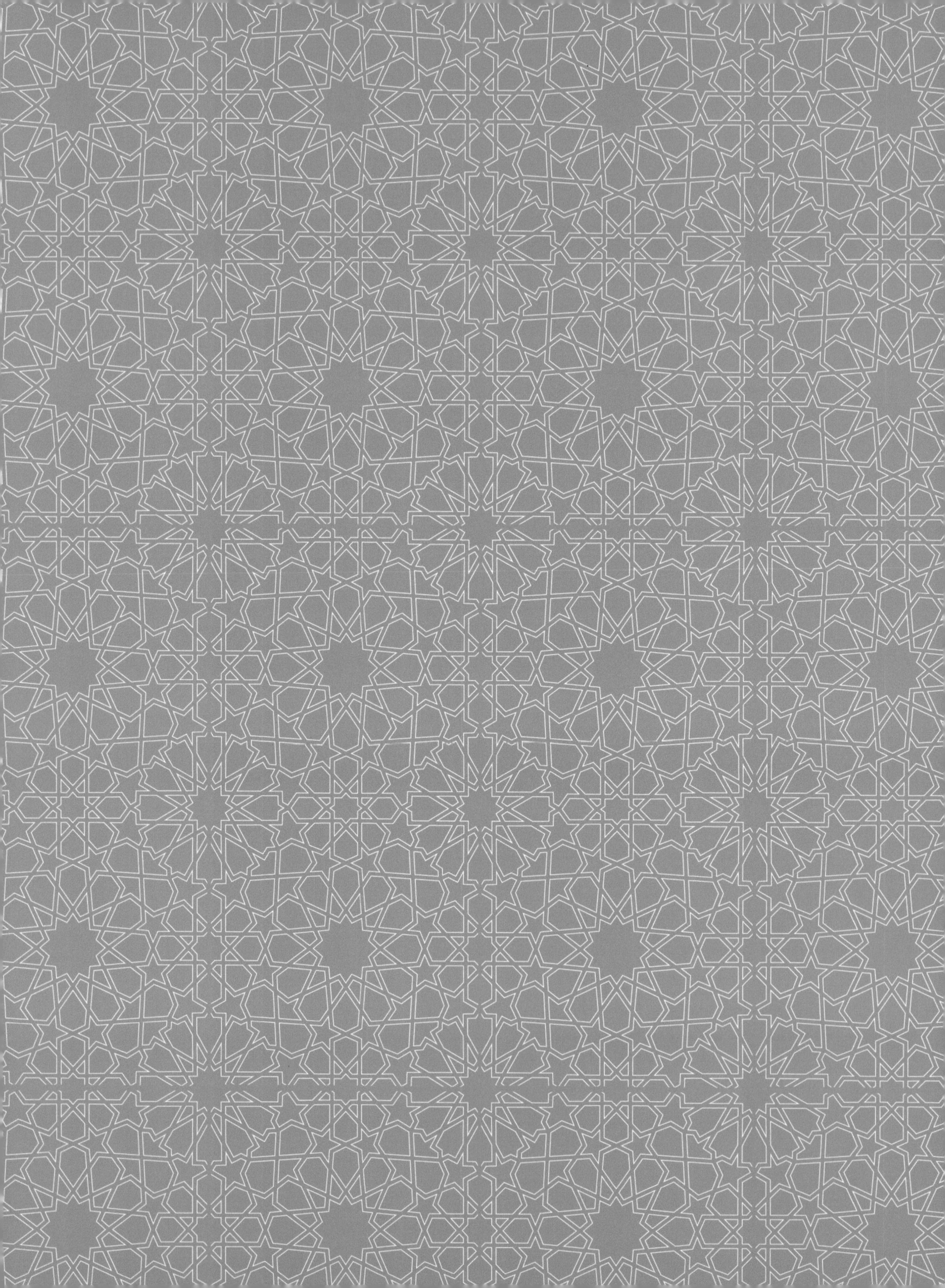

CHAPTER 10

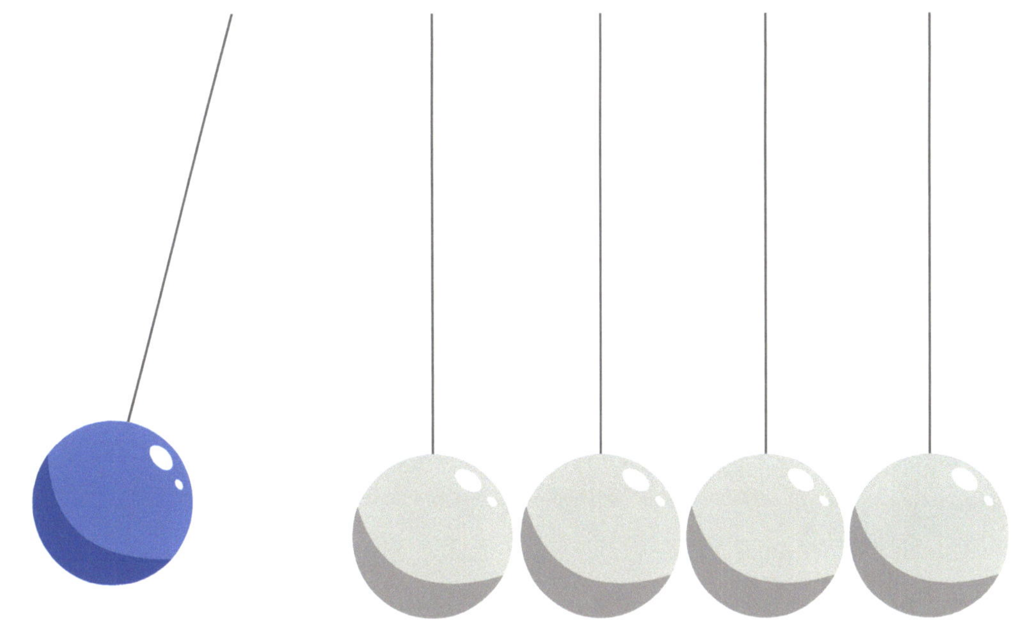

ALLAH'S LAWS OF CAUSE & EFFECT

HIS WILL, HIS WAY

Imagine the following scenario. Your mom reminds you to study for your final exam and you respond, *"I don't need to study because Allah's in control of everything! If He wills, I will pass and if He doesn't, I won't. So I'll just make du'aa."* Will that work? As you may guess, no, probably not!

Allah has created the universe such that it is governed by the laws of cause and effect. For example, Allah is perfectly capable of growing trees and crops without sending down rain, but He chose to make rain a means by which plants grow. He also made medicine a cause for cure, diligence and perseverance a cause for success, work a cause of earning money, and so on. He has instructed us to exert effort and take these means which He provided us with. For example, the Prophet *sallAllahu 'alayhi wa sallam* instructed us to treat our illnesses with medicine:

تَدَاوَوْا فَإِنَّ اللّٰهَ عَزَّ وَجَلَّ لَمْ يَضَعْ دَاءً
إِلاَّ وَضَعَ لَهُ دَوَاءً غَيْرَ دَاءٍ وَاحِدٍ الْهَرَمُ

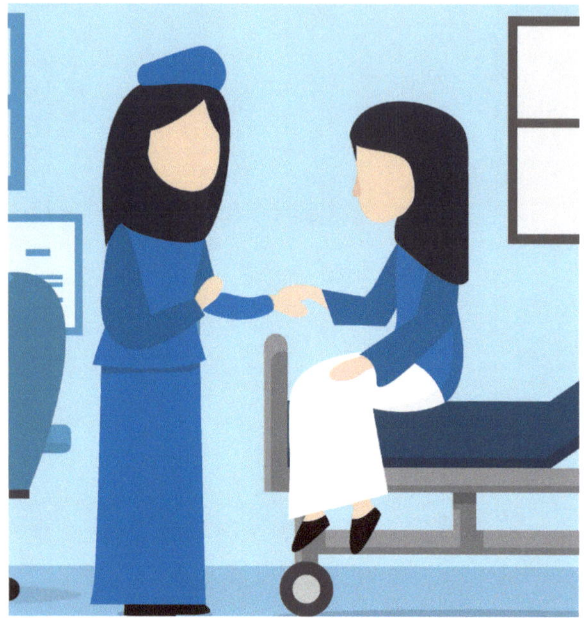

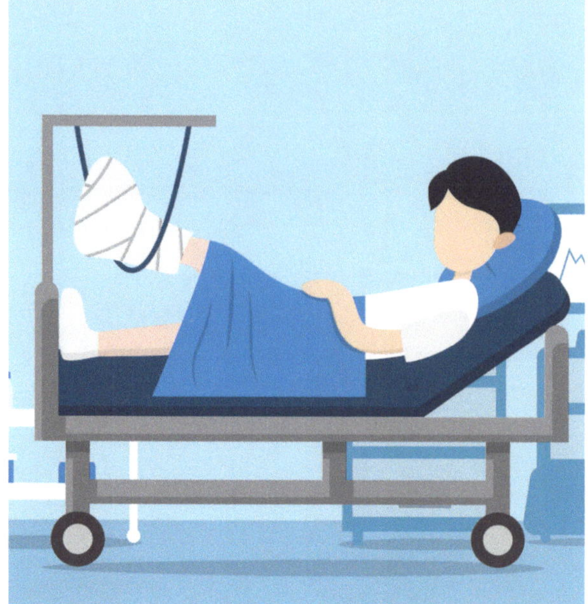

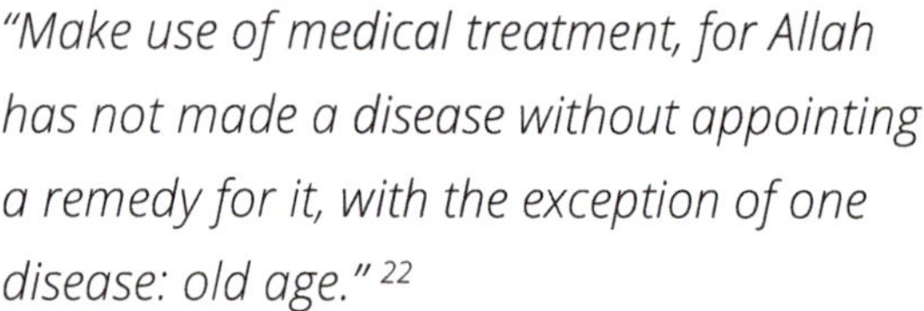

"Make use of medical treatment, for Allah has not made a disease without appointing a remedy for it, with the exception of one disease: old age." [22]

However, it is also important for us to understand that Allah is the One who creates the cause, provides us with it, and makes it effective. A strong belief in Allah's *ruboobiyyah* will cause you to seek help from Allah (*isti'anah*[23]) in each situation. It will also cause you only to rely on Allah (*tawakkul*[24]) throughout the situation, and thank Allah sincerely afterwards. So let's say you studied very hard for a test, and you ended up getting a high score.

You'll have to remember that not everyone who studied hard necessarily got the same result. You could have studied hard but fallen sick, found difficulty concentrating, simply *"blanked out"* during the exam, or had trouble understanding the material. You may have had personal problems that prevented you from studying hard in the first place despite your sincere intention to do so. In other words, Allah facilitated the means for you, gave you the ability and will, and He made them effective.

Two people may have the same illness and both undergo similar treatments; Person A gets cured and Person B doesn't. You may think it's because the first person had better medical care or a more experienced doctor. We have to remember that even good doctors may make mistakes. Even if the doctor was skilled and made no mistakes, who provided Person A with

---

22. Abu Dawud
23. To seek help from Allah alone. This is considered a great act of worship.
24. To rely and depend on Allah alone. This is an act of worship which is internal (in the heart). Only Allah can see if our hearts are depending on Him alone or not.

that doctor to begin with? Who caused his body to respond to the treatment? Who gave him the finances to enable him to get quality treatment? In the end, we have to understand that Allah is the One who provided the means and that He is also able to provide the solution even if the person had no means at all.

This is why our scholars say, *"Taking the means is an act of obedience to Allah, but relying on them in your heart is a form of shirk."* This simply means that we must believe that the causes are not effective on their own, but only by Allah's permission. He is the One who sends them and makes them effective. The causes are all controlled by Him. He is also able to cause things to happen even with no cause present.

Let's take an analogy. Imagine that your grandmother sends you a generous check as a gift through the mail. The person who happened to deliver the check to your house is the mailman. When you receive it, do you feel grateful to the mailman or to your grandmother? Who do you feel provided you with this great gift? Do you say, *"If it weren't for the mailman, I would have never had this money!"* No. You'd simply feel that the mailman was a middleman simply doing his job by delivering your grandmother's gift. You would thank him if you see him, because the Prophet *sallAllahu 'alayhi wa sallam* said, *"Whoever does not thank people has not thanked Allah."* [25] However, you will attribute the gift to your grandmother and you would feel heartfelt gratitude to her. Similarly, Allah is the One who grants us our many blessings or protects us from harm often by way of the means i.e. the *"middleman."* He uses people and causes situations to help us. By attributing His blessings to the *"middleman"* or others only, then we are being ungrateful to Allah.

Why Do We Have Hardships in Life?

As previously mentioned, the *Rabb* is the one who decrees everything that happens in the universe, be it good or bad. Some people may wonder why Allah, the Most Merciful and Compassionate, would cause evil to occur. Why do people get sick? Why do natural disasters occur? Why is there crime or social injustice?

25. At-Tirmidhi

It is true that Allah is the Most Merciful, but He also has other attributes. Among His names are *Al-'Aleem* (the Most Knowledgeable) and *Al-Hakeem* (the Most Wise). Because these attributes are from the very nature of Allah, we know whatever He wills is according to His knowledge and wisdom. Allah's knowledge and wisdom are infinite while ours are limited. At some stages of our lives, we may understand some of His wisdom and reason behind His actions while at other times, we may not.

It's important to keep in mind that just because we do not understand Allah's *hikmah* (wisdom) sometimes, does not mean it's not there. This is similar to a young toddler's limited understanding to that of his parents. If it were not for their guidance, he or she might play with an electric socket or burn herself touching a hot stove top. As the child grows, so does their understanding. Similarly, as our knowledge of Allah grows, we understand some of the wisdom in what happens to us and around us. So we must believe that since Allah is the Most Merciful and Most Wise, everything He does is for a good reason.

Learning Our Limits: A Prophetic Example

Allah explains the concept of learning our limits to us in the *Qur'an* [26] through an interesting story of Prophet Musa *'alayhis salaam* and a righteous man named Khidr. [27] Allah informed Musa *'alayhis salaam* that His servant Khidr had some knowledge from Allah that Musa *'alayhis salaam* didn't have. Musa *'alayhis salaam* was keen to learn what Khidr knew, so he traveled a long distance to meet him. When Musa *'alayhis salaam* asked Khidr if he could learn from him, Khidr responded, *"You will not be able to bear with me patiently. How can you be patient in matters beyond your knowledge?"*

Musa *'alayhis salaam* promised to be patient and obey Khidr. Khidr then made a condition, to which Musa *'alayhis salaam* agreed: *"If you accompany me, do not question anything I do until I explain it to you myself."*

However, on this journey, Khidr, who was not allowed to do anything unless Allah directly instructed him to, did some things that appeared inappropriate or even unjust. First, when they rode a boat, Khidr made a hole in it. Musa *'alayhis salaam* was naturally disturbed, so he immediately said, *"How could you have made a hole in it? Do you want to drown its passengers? What a strange thing to do!"* Khidr reminded Musa *'alayhis*

---

26. Surah Al-Kahf [18:60-82]
27. Some scholars believe Khidr was a prophet because he received revelation from Allah, while others believe he was only a righteous man whom Allah inspired with revelation.

salaam of his promise, so he apologized and they continued on.

Next, Khidr saw a young boy and killed him! Musa *'alayhis salaam* was aghast. *"How could you possibly kill an innocent person who hasn't killed anyone?! What a terrible thing to do!"* Khidr again reminded Musa *'alayhis salaam* of the promise and Musa *'alayhis salaam* again apologized. Musa *'alayhis salaam* said, *"If I question anything again, you can stop me from accompanying you."* Lastly, they arrived at a town and asked the residents for food, but they refused to offer the travelers even the slightest hospitality. Despite this, when Khidr saw a wall that was about to collapse in the town, he repaired it at no cost. Musa *'alayhis salaam* said in astonishment, not necessarily a question, but he could not resist to comment, *"But if you wished, you could have taken a payment for doing this."* At this point, Khidr informed Musa *'alayhis alaam* that they would have to part ways and that he would now explain the reasons for what he did, clarifying that He only did it as per Allah's instruction and not from his own accord.

Khidr explained the three situations accordingly. First of all, there was an oppressive king who was forcibly taking all boats that were in good condition, and this particular boat belonged to a group of poor people and it was their only source of income. So it was best to make a defect in it that could be repaired, so that the king would not want to take it.

He told Musa *'alayhis salaam* that the young boy he killed would have grown up to be a rebellious disbeliever and would eventually lead his parents to disbelief as well. So Allah wished to protect their faith and to replace them with a righteous, compassionate child instead.

He then went on to explain that he repaired the wall, because it belonged to two orphan boys and that there was some wealth buried under the wall for them. Furthermore, their father had been

a righteous man, and knowing the type of people that were in that town that they saw refused to host guests, Allah wanted to protect the wealth of the young boys until they were older.

In all of these cases, this was Allah's decree and Khidr was just the means by which Allah had His decree carried out. In each situation what appeared to be bad was actually good and done out of Allah's mercy for His servants. It shows how Allah takes care of the believer's faith (like in the case of the boy's parents) and their daily, worldly affairs (like in the cases of the ship's owners and the orphans).

This important principle is summarized by Allah in the *Qur'an*,

"...You may dislike something while it is in fact good for you, and you may like something while it is in fact bad for you. And Allah knows but you do not know." [28]

Similarly, the Prophet *sallAllahu 'alayhi wa sallam* said, *"The (situation of) the believer is amazing! Allah does not decree anything for him except if it is good for him."* [29]

So even if something appears evil, it is not pure evil because, in reality, it is for a good reason. One of our scholars, Ibn Taymiyyah *rahimahullah*, explained, *"Allah never creates pure evil; rather, there is a wise and good purpose for everything He creates. Even if there is evil in it for some people, it is only partial, relative evil. However, Allah is far above creating total or absolute evil."* [30] Also, it's important to note, any evil actions we see committed are only one side of the equation. Everyone will be held accountable for their evil actions if they have not sought forgiveness.

---

28. Surah Al-Baqarah [2:216]
29. Ahmad
30. Majmu' Al-Fatawah

Wisdom in Trials

Allah decrees for each person what He knows is good for his or her specific situation. There are also general reasons that Allah allows evil (or what appears evil) to occur, which include:

TO REMIND US OF ALLAH

Our purpose is to worship Him alone. We can only truly achieve peace by doing so. If we never experience any suffering and only experience pleasure, we will forget about Allah and our purpose to worship Him. However, when we are tested, we come closer to Allah by praying to Him more sincerely, seeking His help, and hoping for His mercy. These are all great acts of worship which make our hearts close to our Lord. When He relieves our problems, we feel that He is with us and feel grateful to Him.

THIS LIFE IS A TEST

Allah has informed us of the fact that this world was never intended to be a Paradise, where all of our desires will be fulfilled. Just like in school or university, you cannot be successful or achieve a degree without hard work, challenges, and tests, the same applies to our world. For example, if someone wants to become a brain surgeon, can he or she achieve this easily while partying, spending all his or her time on social media, binge-watching on Netflix, or all of the above? Or does he or she have to make some sacrifices, work hard, and study for many tests? In the end, the achievements of those who spent their entire lives enjoying themselves will be far different than those who endured different trials to achieve their goals.

Similarly, this world is a temporary residence which transitions us into our true and eternal home: Paradise. Allah tells us,

ٱلَّذِى خَلَقَ ٱلْمَوْتَ وَٱلْحَيَوٰةَ لِيَبْلُوَكُمْ أَيُّكُمْ أَحْسَنُ عَمَلًا

"(He is) the one who created death and life to test you as to who is best in deeds." [31]

He also informs us,

وَنَبْلُوكُم بِٱلشَّرِّ وَٱلْخَيْرِ فِتْنَةً ۖ وَإِلَيْنَا تُرْجَعُونَ

"And We test you with both good and evil as a trial, and you will return to Us." [32]

When good happens, Allah is testing us to see if we will worship Him alone by recognizing that this good was only from Him and thank Him for it. And if bad happens, He is testing us to see if we believe in our hearts that it is for our benefit and is out of His mercy and wisdom, and if, in turn, we will trust Him and be patient. Passing these tests will cause us to enter Paradise, where there will be no tests, stress, sadness, grief, or anxiety - only bliss and complete relief. Surely such a great eternal reward cannot come easily! These tests help detach us from this world and make us look forward to Paradise and work harder for it.

GRATITUDE

If a person never experienced sickness, he or she will take their health for granted. Similarly, if a person never experiences hard times, he or she may not even recognize good times. This causes us to be grateful to Allah for all that He has given us.

KNOWING ALLAH

When we are battling any illness, we understand that only Allah is the Healer. When we discover that a bad situation turned out to be for our best interest, we understand that Allah is the Most Wise and Knowing. When He protects us from our fears, we understand that He is the only Protector. When we receive any blessing or success, we realize that He is the Most Merciful and Most Generous. When we pray for our difficulty to be removed and He responds, we realize that He is the Most Able and the only one who hears and responds to our prayers. This only increases our love for Him and closeness to Him.

---

31. Surah Al-Mulk [67:2]
32. Surah Al-Anbiyaa [21:35]

FORGIVENESS AND HIGHER LEVELS IN PARADISE

Prophet Muhammad *sallAllahu 'alayhi wa sallam* said, *"Whenever a believer is afflicted with any discomfort, illness, anxiety, grief, harm, or mental worry, even if he were simply pricked by a thorn, Allah will erase some of his sins because of it."* [33] The Prophet *sallAllahu 'alayhi wa sallam* also said, *"The greatness of the reward is based on the severity of the trial. So when Allah loves people, He tries them."* [34]

REFINEMENT AND ELEVATION OF CHARACTER

High temperatures and pressure transform a rock into a diamond in billions of years. *Alhamdulillah,* it doesn't take quite that long for human characters to strengthen and shine. However, it is well known that trials strengthen people's characters. Through trials, we gain character traits such as determination, patience, courage, compassion, empathy, and humility. Similarly, trials rid us of our bad qualities like arrogance, insensitivity, selfishness, and cowardice.

33. Sahih Al-Bukhari
34. At-Tirmidhi

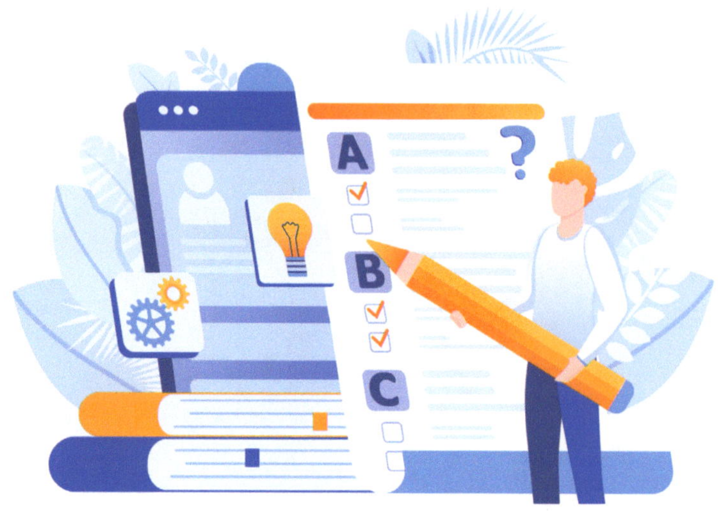

CHAPTER 10

REVIEW AND REFLECT QUESTIONS

1

Some people believe that if bad things happen to them, then it means that Allah doesn't love them. How would you explain to such a person that this isn't necessarily the case.

2

Allah's special *tarbiyah* in the lives of the prophets can be very inspiring when you hear about the struggles they had to experience and the guidance that they received to overcome. Think about a time in your life when you felt inspired and motivated to take a course of action despite it being at a difficult time.

3

What do you think will happen when you choose to act with the intention of seeking Allah's love and pleasure instead of focusing on other people's love and acceptance?

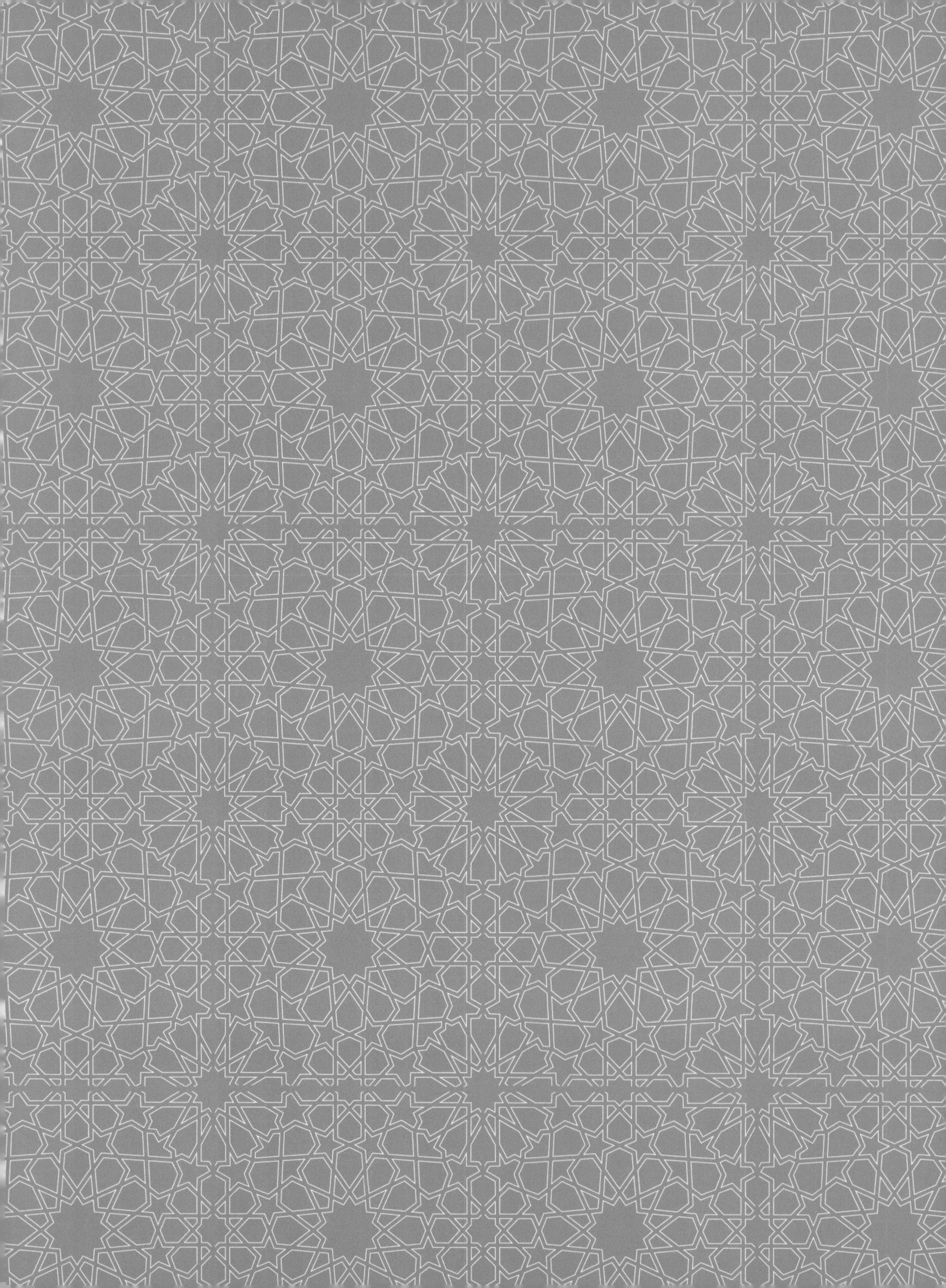

CHAPTER 11

COMMON MISTAKES IN BELIEF

Shirk in Ruboobiyyah

THE DANGERS OF *SHIRK*

Shirk means to associate a partner to Allah or make someone an equal to Him whether by raising a creation's status too high (similar to what the Christians did with Prophet 'Isa *'alayhis salaam*) or lowering that of our Rabb (similar to some of Judaism's beliefs when it comes to characteristics of our Creator). This is the opposite of *tawheed*, which is a firm belief in Allah's oneness. *Shirk* is very dangerous, because it is considered the worst sin in the eyes of Allah. Essentially, it is giving credit to someone else for what Allah has done for us. It goes against our very nature, and the reason for which we were created to begin with. Allah says,

إِنَّ ٱلشِّرْكَ لَظُلْمٌ عَظِيمٌ

"Truly shirk is a great injustice." [35]

35. Surah Luqman [31:13]

ACTIVITY

Can you think of various ways people give credit to others instead of Allah?

BRAIN TEASER

What are the implications of the ways in which people give credit to other things such as "*karma*" or "*the Universe*"? Is this *shirk*? Why or why not?

The Prophet *sallAllahu 'alayhi wa sallam* said,

أَلَا أُنَبِّئُكُمْ بِأَكْبَرِ الْكَبَائِرِ. قُلْنَا بَلَى يَا رَسُولَ اللَّهِ. قَالَ الإِشْرَاكُ بِاللَّهِ

"Should I inform you of the absolute greatest sin? It is to set up an equal with Allah..." [36]

If a person repents from *shirk* in this life, he or she will be forgiven *in shaa Allah*. However, if someone dies without repenting from *shirk,* it is the only sin which Allah will not forgive on the Day of Judgment.

Allah informs us,

إِنَّ ٱللَّهَ لَا يَغْفِرُ أَن يُشْرَكَ بِهِۦ وَيَغْفِرُ مَا دُونَ ذَٰلِكَ لِمَن يَشَآءُ وَمَن يُشْرِكْ بِٱللَّهِ فَقَدْ ضَلَّ ضَلَٰلًا بَعِيدًا

"Certainly, Allah does not forgive associating a partner (shirk) with Him, but He forgives what is less than that for whom He wills. And he who has associated a partner to Allah has gone far astray." [37]

Why is *Shirk* Dangerous?

What makes *shirk* such a grave sin? Let's look at an analogous example in this life. Imagine that someone has a caring mother. This mother gave birth to him, took care of him, and provided him with all his needs including feeding him, clothing him and giving him all the necessary medical and nutritional needs. She also fulfilled all of his emotional needs by being kind and compassionate. She made all decisions in his best interest, weighing them carefully and wisely. She provided him with the best education and gave him all the support he needed.

36. Sahih Muslim
37. Surah An-Nisaa [04:116]

One day, when he got older, he told her, *"As far as I'm concerned, you're not my mother."* He left her, never communicated with her, and acted as if she did not exist. He did not respond to any of her calls or listen to any of her reminders. To make matters worse, he decided that an absolute stranger, who had done nothing for him, will get the care and loyalty that his mother deserved. Even if this person were to be kind to others, it would be in vain because he denied the most important person in his life - the very person who brought him into the world cared for him tirelessly, and provided him with everything he has.

Of course, we cannot compare anyone to Allah, not even the mother, but this simply provides an example to bring the idea closer to home. Similarly, if we credit *"mother nature," "the universe,"* or signs and good luck charms instead of attributing it to Allah, we are no different in our attitude towards Allah as the child in the above example was to his mother. This is *shirk,* which is associating partners with Allah, and there are two types.

THE TWO TYPES OF *SHIRK*

1. MAJOR *SHIRK*
2. MINOR *SHIRK*

MAJOR *SHIRK*

This kind of *shirk* is the one we just discussed. It takes the person out of the fold of Islam and results in an eternity in the Hellfire.

MINOR *SHIRK*

This type of *shirk* is a major sin, but it does not take the person out of Islam.

1. MAJOR *SHIRK* IN *RUBOOBIYYAH*

This includes believing that someone or something other than Allah created the universe or that the universe has no creator. Believing that someone other than Allah can control the universe and decree what happens in it is a major *shirk* in Allah's *Ruboobiyyah*. It also includes the belief that angels, prophets, saints, spirits, imams or righteous people can control or affect the events of this life, even after their deaths. It also includes the belief that charms can bring good or bad fortune.

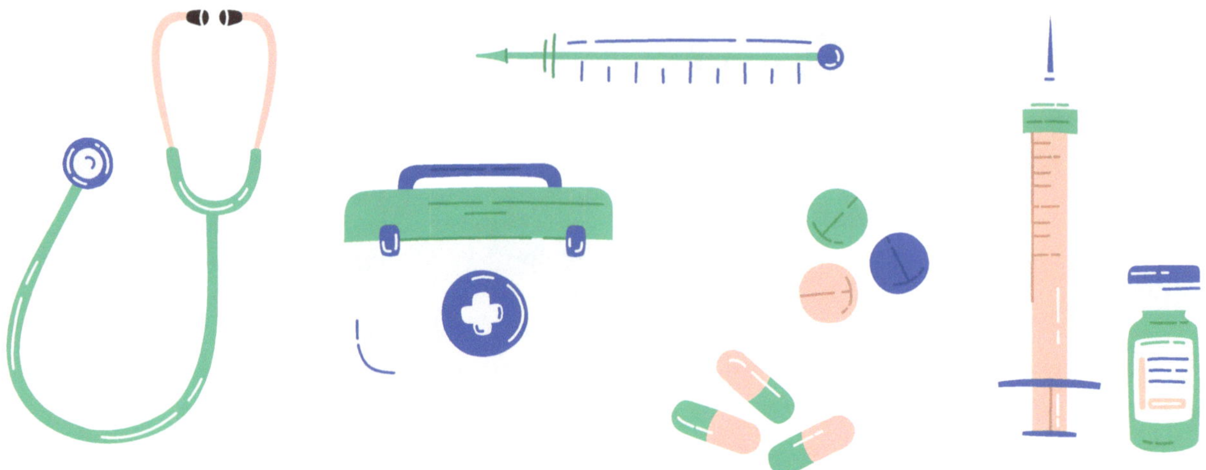

2. MINOR *SHIRK* IN *RUBOOBIYYAH*

It is a minor *shirk* to attribute good or bad to other than Allah. For example, if a doctor completed a successful surgery and the patient then said, *"If it weren't for the doctor, I would have died,"* believing that the doctor was truly the only cause of his cure, it can be a form of minor *shirk*. He should instead say, *"If it weren't for Allah, then the doctor, I would have died"* or *"If it weren't for the doctor's success, by Allah's permission, I would have died,"* or simply, *"If it weren't for Allah, I would have died."* This is tricky, because it doesn't have to be said explicitly either. That's why it is important to look inwards at ourselves and question whether we are committing even minor forms of *shirk*. Some questions to ask ourselves: Am I overly praising or admiring someone? What do I think about that distracts me from Allah? If I don't feel concentration in my *salaah*, where does my mind go? Which part of the *deen* do I feel I compromise on? Do I carry arrogance in my heart? Could I be attributing any success I have in my life to myself?

Can you identify some examples of major *shirk* in our society today? How about examples of minor *shirk*?

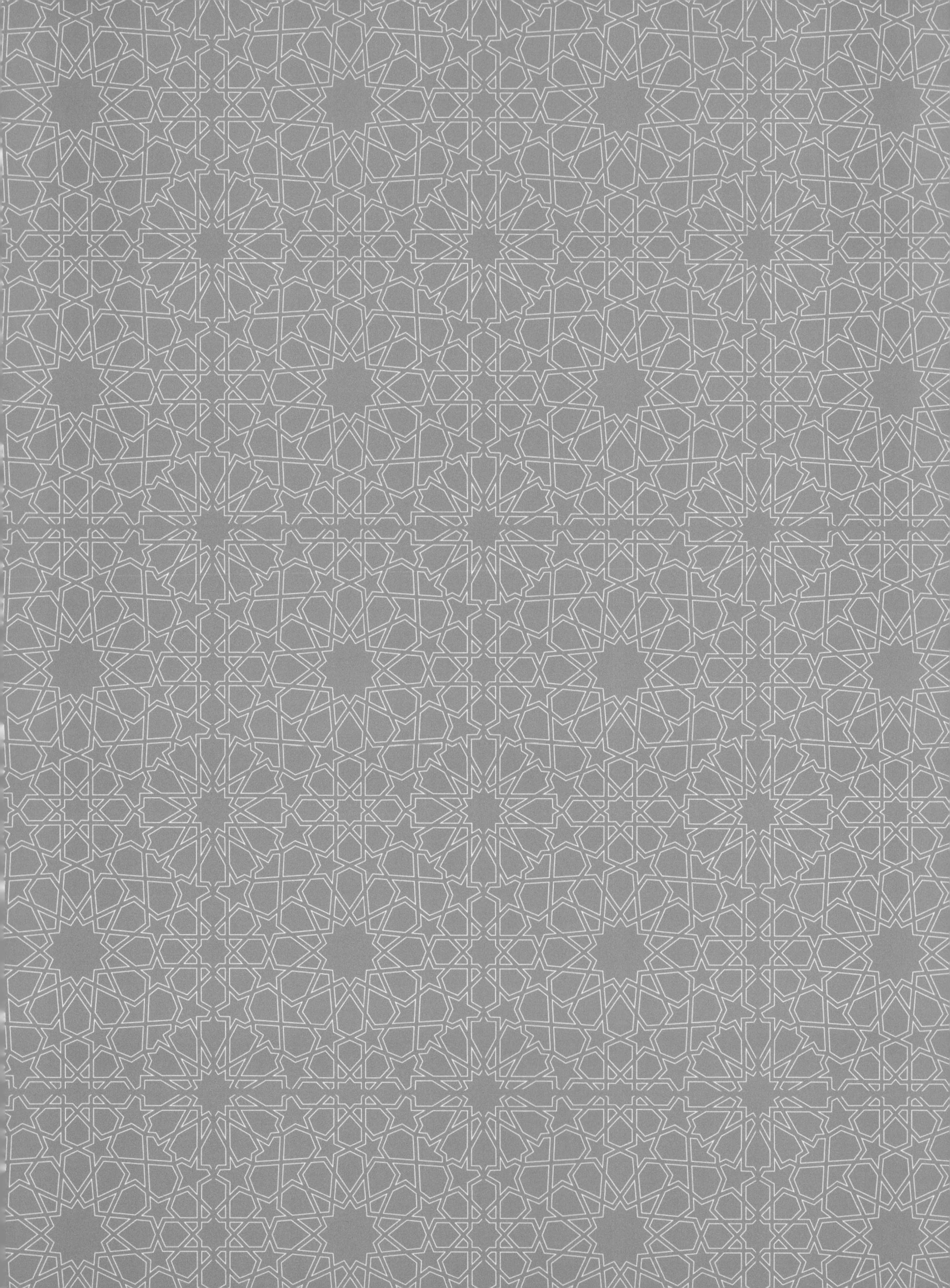

CHAPTER 12

TAWHEED IN OUR EVERYDAY LIFE

TAWHEED AND EMOTIONAL WELL-BEING

Sometimes we feel disappointed or even depressed if we do not get enough attention from others at a gathering or via social media. However, if our main concern is to please Allah. As discussed earlier, we should not worry about people's love and acceptance. We should focus only on Allah's love and acceptance. So if your main concern is to please Him rather than His creation, He will cause people to love and respect you.

TAWHEED AND DECISION MAKING

Let's say you are at a crossroad in life. It could be planning your major or choosing between a difficult situation. Or, it could be a simpler life decision like whether you should attend an event or choosing between two flights. Naturally, you want to make the best decision and avoid anything harmful. How can you make the best decision? Have strong confidence that Allah is the *Rabb,* who controls everything, big and small. He takes special care of His believers and He will guide you to what is best for you.

PROPER STEPS TO DECISION **MAKING**

1 ***DU'AA***

You would first turn to Him, seek His help, and ask Him for guidance on how you'll achieve your goal.

---

2 **BRAINSTORMING**

Then you start planning all the possible ways you can to achieve your objective.

---

3 ***ISTIKHARAH***

Ask Allah to guide you by praying a special prayer for guidance, *salaat-ul-istikharah* *, as to whether or not this step is good for you. You must believe that only He knows which choice will be best.

---

*Refer to page 130 to learn how to perform it.

4

ISTISHARAH

Do your research and consult with trustworthy people with relevant experience, and correct understanding of the *Qur'an* and *Sunnah*.

5

IMPLEMENTING

Then you start implementing your plan and actively working to achieve your goal.

6

TAWAKKUL

Knowing wholeheartedly that Allah is the only One who will grant you success. True *Tawakku*l is relying on Allah alone and it is considered a great act of worship.

7

GRATITUDE

You will either win or learn thus be grateful to Allah. Any success is from Allah and if the result is not as we hoped, we know Allah is the best of planners and there is wisdom in it. Perhaps it is a mercy of Allah that it did not happen.

8

ISTI'ANAH

Remember, as discussed earlier, a strong belief in Allah's *Ruboobiyyah* will cause you to seek help from Allah inwardly *(isti'anah)* and to rely and depend on Allah alone *(tawakkul)*. This is an act of worship that exists internally in the heart. Only Allah can see if our hearts are depending on Him alone.

HOW TO PERFORM SALAAT-UL-ISTIKHARA?

To make *salaat-ul-istikhara,* pray 2 *rakaat* voluntary or supererogatory *(sunnah* or *nafl)* prayers and then recite the following *du'a* while sitting in the last *raka'h,* just before saying the *salaam.*

فَإِنَّك تَقْدِر وَلَا أَقْدِر وَتَعْلَم وَلَا أَعْلَم وَأَنْت عَلَّام الْغُيُوب

اللَّهُمَّ إِنْ كُنْت تَعْلَم أَن هَذَا الْأَمْرخَيْر لِي فِي دِينِي وَمَعَاشِي وَعَاقِبَةِ أَمْري

فَاقْدُرْهُ لِي وَيَسِّرْهُ لِي ثُمَّ بَارِكْ لِي فِيه

وَإِنْ كُنْتَ تَعْلَم أَنَّ هَذَا الْأَمْر شَرٌّ لِي فِي دِينِي وَمَعَاشِي وَعَاقِبَةِ أَمْرِي

فَاصْرِفْهُ عَنِّي وَاصْرِفْنِي عَنْهُ وَاقْدُرْ لِيَ الْخَيْرَ حَيْث كَانَ ثُمَّ أَرْضِنِي بِه

O Allah! I ask guidance from Your knowledge, And Power from Your Might and I ask for Your great blessings. You are capable and I am not. You know and I do not know and You know the unseen. O Allah! If You know that this (mention the issue, need or matter in the *du'a* after the phrase; " هَذَا الْأَمْر ") is good for my religion and my sustenance and in my Hereafter.

Then You ordain it for me and make it easy for me to get, And then bless me in it, and if You know that this (mention the issue, need or matter in the *du'a* after the phrase; " هَذَا الْأَمْر ") is harmful to me In my religion and my sustenance and in the Hereafter. Then keep it away from me and let me be away from it. And ordain for me whatever is good for me, And make me satisfied with it.

CHAPTER 12

REVIEW AND REFLECT QUESTIONS

Evaluate the different scenarios below.
What mistakes in Ruboobiyyah do you see in each?

1

A student you know in middle school is being bullied. She feels helpless and decides that there is no point in talking to anyone or doing anything about it, but instead she will only make dua. What is wrong in this scenario?

2

One day, a popular high schooler sees the bullying incident, defends the student, and threatens the bully. The student says with full conviction, *"I am so grateful to this high school student! If it wasn't for her, I would have never had a way out."* What might be wrong with this thinking or statement?

3

A family friend who lives in Virginia wants to visit her family in Egypt. She has looked at tickets and the most affordable one is on Friday the 13th. She refuses to travel that day out of fear of bad luck, and looks for tickets that are much more expensive but on a different day. How would you advise this woman in this situation?

4

Your friend has been studying very hard for her SAT exam. She gets nervous and prays two rak'aat before beginning her exam. She then grabs a bracelet she wore when she scored well on her final exams for good luck. How is this disobedience to Allah?

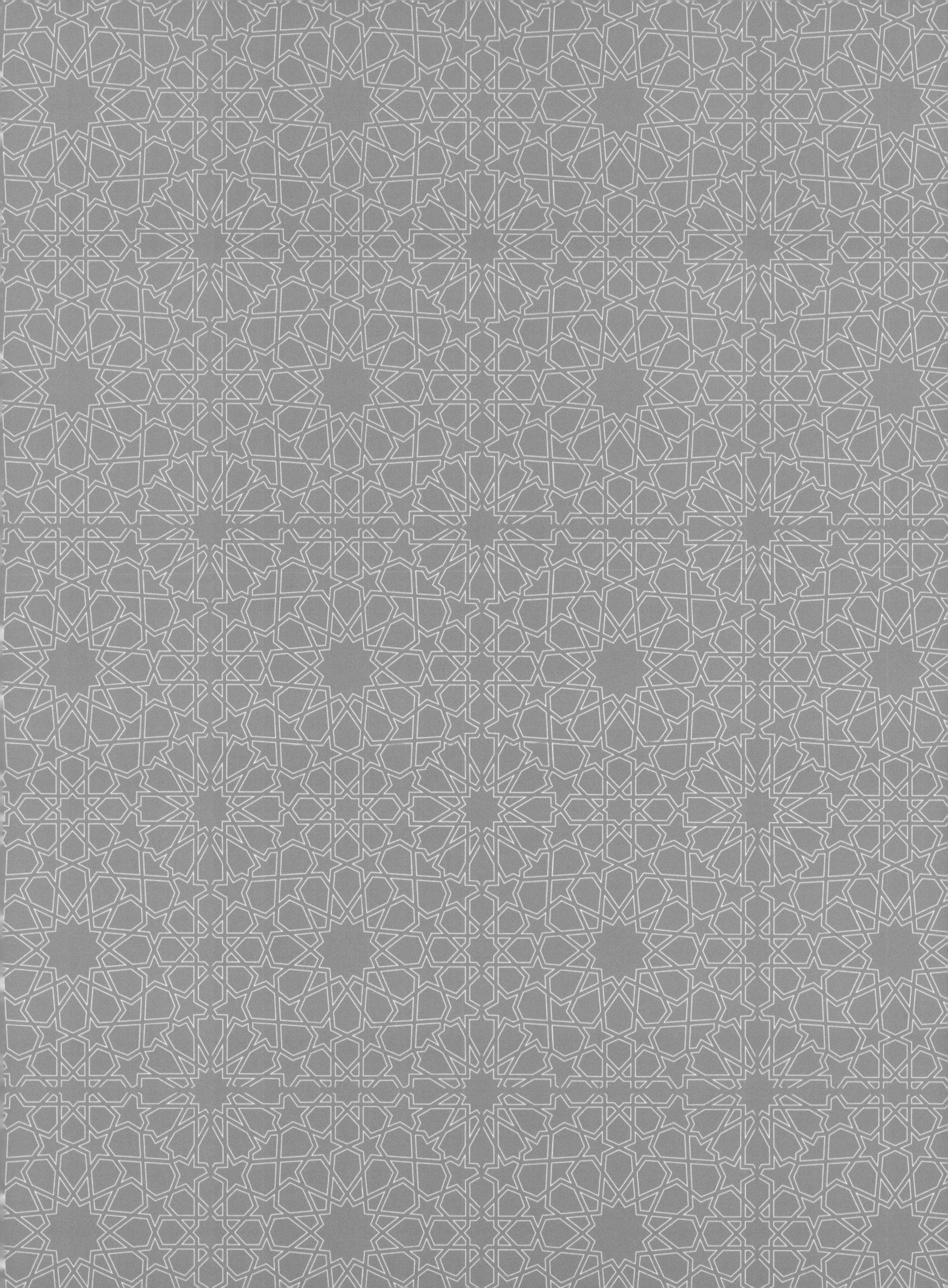

FREQUENTLY USED EXPRESSIONS

1 SALLALLAHU ‘ALAYHI WA SALLAM

May Allah's peace and blessings be upon him.

This is the *du'aa* that Allah has asked us to make whenever the name of the Prophet Muhammad *sallAllahu 'alayhi wa sallam* is mentioned. Allah commands us,

"Indeed, Allah confers blessing upon the Prophet, and His angels (ask Him to do so).

O you who have believed, ask (Allah to confer) blessing upon him and ask (Allah to grant him) peace." [38]

The Prophet *sallAllahu 'alayhi wa sallam* also told us,

"The one who offers salah for me from my Ummah, sincerely from their heart, Allah will then offer ten salahs for them, will raise them ten degrees, write for them ten good deeds, and cancel for them ten sins." [39]

2 'ALAYHIS SALAAM

May Allah's peace be on him.

This expression is a *du'aa* which is used whenever referring to a Prophet of Allah other than Prophet Muhammad *sallAllahu 'alayhi wa sallam*.

3 RADHIALLAHU ‘ANHU

May Allah be pleased with him.

This expression is a *du'aa* which is usually used whenever referring to a companion of the Prophet Muhammad *sallAllahu 'alayhi wa sallam.*

---

38. Surah Al-Ahzab [33:56]
39. Al-Nasa'i, declared Sahih by Al-Albani

www.ingramcontent.com/pod-product-compliance
Lightning Source LLC
LaVergne TN
LVHW070127110826
845147LV00002B/204
9798987400654